History of Modern Thought

Other Books by the Same Author

FORMAL LOGIC

EPISTEMOLOGY

CARTESIANISM

Published by
FORDHAM UNIVERSITY PRESS
NEW YORK, NEW YORK

HISTORY

OF

MODERN THOUGHT

The English, Irish and Scotch Schools

BY

MICHAEL J. MAHONY, S.J., Ph.D., LL.D.

FORDHAM UNIVERSITY

FORDHAM UNIVERSITY PRESS
NEW YORK
1933

Imprimi Potest

EDUARDUS C. PHILLIPS, S.J.
Praep. Prov. Provinciae Marylandiae — Neo Eboracensis

Nihil Obstat

ARTHUR J. SCANLAN, S.T.D.
Censor Librorum

Imprimatur

✠ PATRICK CARDINAL HAYES
Archbishop of New York

NEW YORK, March 10, 1933

Preface

THIS little book which is a sequel to "Cartesianism" is not written for professional philosophers. Its less ambitious purpose is to initiate undergraduate students of Catholic Universities and Colleges, who are engaged in the study of scholastic philosophy, into a knowledge of the fundamental principles of those numerous systems that have contributed to the chaos of modern thought from the time of Descartes to the present day. Frankly stated the postulates underlying this study of modern thought are, that scholasticism is, on the one hand, not merely a philosophy among philosophies, but that it is the only philosophy that has assimilated the wisdom of the ages, that it is ready to acknowledge whatever may be true in other systems, that it comes closest among all rivals to the possession of absolute truth, and that it is not stereotyped or immobile but capable of adapting itself to all modern needs, whereas, on the other hand, it is difficult to conceive how any thoughtful mind with a sense of humor could accept any one of the numerous systems that have appeared since the seventeenth century, except in an attitude of easy-going scepticism, because of their ephemeral and mutually contradictory characters. Still the study of modern thought is not only profitable, but is to-day a necessary complement to the adequate study of scholasticism, not indeed on account of the intrinsic value of so many modern doctrines, but rather that the principles of modern thinkers may be *contrasted* with the positions of Scholasticism. *Contrast* is the watchword in the comparative study of scholasticism and modern thought. The lustre of a diamond is enhanced by the interposition of darker shades.

The solutions offered by modern thinkers to so many philosophical problems are in direct conflict with the solutions of scholasticism. Hence a strong conviction that no student can have an adequate grasp of scholasticism unless he also knows modern philosophy, is forced upon anyone who has spent some years in the teaching of both. For instance a class may know that Kant accounts for the universality and necessity of scientific knowledge by the theory that these characteristics come from out the mind itself. Should the class, then, be asked, how does scholasticism account for these characteristics? Rarely, if ever, is any answer forthcoming. Again a class may learn that Descartes made consciousness the starting point of knowledge. Then the question is asked, what cognitive faculty do you make the starting point of knowledge? Blank faces usually meet the eye. Numerous are such contrasts. If one's philosophy is, then, to become a living force in the conduct of one's life, and a key to the solution of modern needs and conditions, that philosophy must be capable of wrestling successfully with the opposing systems of his times, and of meeting the test of experience and emerging unchanged out of every form of fair discussion.

M. J. M., S.J.

TABLE OF CONTENTS

THE ENGLISH, IRISH AND SCOTCH SCHOOLS

Introduction

JOHN LOCKE, George Berkeley, and David Hume — an Englishman, an Irishman, and a Scotchman — these three are the mountain peaks in the landscape of the earlier schools of modern thought in the English speaking world.

The materialistic Hobbes and the empirical Bacon, indeed, preceded Locke, and prepared the data of his philosophy. But the stream of influence that is typical of modern English thought flowed, not from Hobbes or Bacon but from Locke. Neither Hobbes nor Bacon founded a school. Intellectually Locke dominated his century. The problems propounded, but left unsolved by Locke, challenged the ingenuity of the philosophical world of the seventeenth and eighteenth centuries to offer its solutions. The more logical Berkeley reduced Locke's System to Idealism; the keen, canny mind of Hume brought both the philosophy of Locke and Berkeley to the despair of universal scepticism. Even intimations of Kant may be discovered in the philosophy of Locke.

To know, then, in its initial stages the origin and temper of the national thought of England, and the characteristic tendencies of modern English and American thought today, we ought to become familiar with the root-principles of Locke's philosophy, just as it was necessary to know Descartes, in order to grasp intelligently the curious developments of the Cartesian thought-systems. "He who considers things in their growth and origin," says Aristotle, "will obtain the clearest view of them."

It would be a mistake, however, to imagine that Locke, Berkeley and Hume had no intellectual affinity with Descartes and the Cartesians. "Cartesianism is an essential element in the philosophical and moral history of modern

times."[1]   It was undoubtedly Descartes that inspired
Locke — "He often told me," says Lady Masham "that
the first books that gave him a relish for philosophical
reading were those of Descartes."[2]   Kuno Fisher regarded
Cartesianism, and the antinomies into which it enters as
it develops, as the origin and necessary condition of the
Occasionalism (and Ontologism) of Malebranche, the Mon-
ism of Spinoza, the monadology of Leibnitz, the Sensual-
ism of Locke, the Materialism of Lamettrie, the Idealism
of Berkeley, (the Phenomenalism of Hume) and the Criticism of Kant."[3]   Hence Balmes could justly say that, "it
was neither in Germany nor England, but in Catholic
France, that the philosophical movement advanced with
the greatest freedom and daring.   Descartes, the founder
of a new era in philosophy that superseded the Aristotelian, and gave a fresh impulse to the study of logic, of
physics, and metaphysics, was a Frenchman and a Catholic. The greater part of his most distinguished followers
were also in communion with the Church of Rome. Philosophy, then, in the highest sense of the word, owes
nothing to Protestantism.   Before Leibnitz, Germany
could scarcely reckon a single philosopher of note; and
the English Schools that attained to anything like celeb-
rity arose after Descartes' time. We shall find upon reflection that France was the centre of the philosophical
movement from the end of the sixteenth century, and at
that period all the Protestant countries were so backward
in that kind of study, that the active progress of philosophy amongst the Catholics was scarcely noticed by
them."[4]

When the Cartesian philosophy awakened and inspired
the mind of Locke to devote himself to philosophical investigations, that philosophy in its reception by a mentality characteristically English, was so transformed, that
it manifested itself in a system very different from that

[1]Emile Boutroux—"Historical Studies in Phil." p. 236.
[2]"John Locke—Modern Philosophies" p. 5.
[3]Emile Boutroux—Ibid., p. 234.
[4]Protestantism and Catholicism, C. LXXII, p. 417.

which the French genius of Descartes gave to the world.
"Quidquid recipitur, secundum modum recipientis recipitur." Descartes unduly emphasized the intellectual and
minimized the sense elements in human knowledge. Indeed in Descartes' epistemology there is no place for sense
knowledge properly so-called. Recall his doctrine of "innate
ideas," which arise from the depths of the pure, spiritual
soul without being caused by any efficient determination
of the external reality which they professed to represent.
Even the ideas which Descartes calls "adventitious"
spring up somehow in the soul or spirit, which to Descartes was the man, on the *occasion* merely of the mechanical excitation of the "animal spirits." Even the
existence of matter in Descartes' system, is known, not
by any direct sense perception, but by a process of reasoning (and reason is the same faculty as intellect) grounded
on two premises, both of which are innate — the subjective persuasion that matter does exist, and the veracity
of God. Even Descartes' sophistical arguments for the
existence of God are only analytic deductions, mathematical in method, from his innate *idea* of God.

The English mentality of Locke, on the contrary,
which is wedded to the concrete, individual sensuous
"ideas," made known by sense experience, and which are
valid in so far as they can be tested by sense experience,
tends to emphasize unduly sense knowledge, and minimize,
if it does not deny outright, intellectual knowledge. Hence
Locke repudiates the innate ideas of Descartes. Thus
the idea of "substance," because it is directly and "per se"
supersensible, Locke relegates to the realm of the "unknown". It is something merely "supposed or imagined,"[1]
because, forsooth, it is not an object *"per se"* of sense.
"Species," "notion" and "phantasm" he includes under
the same category, that is, he calls them by the same
name — "ideas." Consequently he judges them to be of
the same nature, and thus wipes out the clear-cut, traditional distinction between intellectual (species, notion)

---

[1]Essay, B II, XXII, 2.

and sensuous "ideas" (phantasm)[1]. "In all the great extent," says Locke, "wherein the mind wanders, in those remote speculations it may seem to be elevated with, *it stirs not one jot* beyond those ideas, which sense and reflection (which he calls an internal sense) have offered for its contemplation."[2] Again Locke asserts that, "every man's reasoning and knowledge is only about the ideas existing in his own mind, which are truly, every one of them, *particular existences* — so that the perception of the agreement or disagreement of our particular ideas, is the whole and utmost of all our knowledge. Universality is only accidental to it."[3] Those statements of Locke dispose of all intellectual knowledge in man, and make of him only an animal. Extremes beget extremes. Thus would Descartes make man an angel,[4] and Locke a glorified animal.

Yet Locke seems to be more of an Aristotelian, and consequently more Scholastic than the Platonic Descartes. Yet the Scholasticism that influenced Locke was not that of St. Thomas, nor its brilliant development in Spain in the sixteenth century under the leadership of Suarez and his colleagues, but rather the decadent Scholasticism of Occam, Locke's countryman, who was likewise a Sensist and a Nominalist.

Locke fails to distinguish between sensuous phenomena or phantasms and intellectual, universal concepts. In the face of this failure, it is difficult not to infer the utter paralysis of the intellectual power of reason. How can any mediate inference be drawn by reason, if the only premises given to us must always be particular? Logic demands that reasoning is impossible if one of the premises at least is not universal or equivalent to a universal, that is, taken in all its extension or distributed. Hence the denial of the genuine universality of concepts is the death-blow to any intellectual element in human

[1]Essay, Introd., 8.
[2]Ibid., B II, C I-24.
[3]Ibid., B IV, C XVII-8.
[4]Cf. Maritain, "Three Reformers".

knowledge and the proclamation of Sensism or Sensationalism. If, then, the philosophy of Descartes may
be justly called "exaggerated intellectualism," the philosophy of Locke and his school, is justly characterized in
the history of modern thought, as "exaggerated sensism
or empiricism." Descartes stressed to exaggeration the
intellectual elements in knowledge. Locke exaggerated
the empirical elements in knowledge and practically annihilated the intellectual. If Locke did admit intellectual
elements in human knowledge, they were to him, as they
were to Kant, creations of the mind that gave no insight
into the nature of existing realities. Extremes are never
just or true. Extreme heat kills, so does extreme cold.
Scholastic philosophy which is "wise unto sobriety,"
avoids both extremes by recognizing in human knowledge
both the intellectual and empirical elements. Hence scholasticism steers a moderate "via media" between the ex-
aggerations of Descartes and Locke, and establishes a
system that may be appropriately termed "empirico-intellectualism." But the fashionable philosophers of the
seventeenth and eighteenth centuries looked upon traditional scholasticism as effete and outworn.

In our exposition, then, of the modern thought of
England, we shall first endeavor to explain the root-principles of Locke's Sensism or Empiricism, a system which
narrows the range of human knowledge to *experienced
sensuous facts as the only realities* that man can know.
The supersensible or metempirical realities such as *substance, essence, cause, purposes*, etc., because, forsooth,
we cannot directly and in themselves, see, hear, taste,
touch or smell them, are relegated to the realm of the
unknown, and metaphysics is transformed into a fairyland
of imagined realities. And since the logical implications
embodied in the Sensism of Locke were quickly developed
by his disciples into Idealism, Phenomenalism, Positivism,
Materialism, and Agnosticism, the explanation and criticism of those systems will be included in our study of the
English school.

Nor was the influence of Locke's philosophy, and the

systems which that philosophy enfolded, confined to Great
Britain and Ireland.   The debt of English thought to Descartes was subsequently repaid, in very inferior currency
we fear, by the sympathetic response which Locke's Sensism called forth in France.   Condillac's gross Sensationalism, Compte's Positivism, the Materialism of Lamettrie,
d'Holbach and Diderot were the outcome of Locke's influence upon the more logical French thinkers, systems
which, combined with the irrational license of Descartes'
spirit of free-thought, and his unfortunate break with the
continuity of the traditional philosophy, precipitated the
horrors of the French Revolution.

During the closing years of our colonial period, Materialism, no doubt through the influence of the Lockean
philosophy, was rampant in Philadelphia (Priestley),
in New York (Cadwalder Colden) and in Kentucky
(Buchanan).

Whether motived by a humorous or serious purpose,
Hume, by the force of rigorous logic deduced from the
principles and implications of Locke and Berkeley a system of utter scepticism.   This "reductio ad absurdum"
of the Lockean philosophy at the hands of Hume aroused
on the continent, towards the end of the eighteenth and
at the beginning of the nineteenth century, a violent reaction against English Empiricism.   A like reaction had
set in against Cartesianism — the only recognized, contemporary rival of Empiricism in the philosophical world.
Scholasticism was of course, ignored by the dominant
schools.   Both Descartes' and Locke's perverted accounts
of human knowledge called for a remedy and reform.   To
institute this reform, a new luminary in the philosophical
world appeared in Germany — Emmanuel Kant, who was
hailed as the "new Aristotle" of modern thought.   It was
Kant's laudable ambition to elaborate a new system which
was to be built upon the ruins to which Hume reduced
the doctrines of Locke and his disciples, and, at the same
time remedy the inadequacy of Cartesianism.   Kant saw
clearly that there were intellectual elements of genuine
universality and necessity inherent in human knowledge

that could not be eliminated, and that these essential elements, the sensuous Empiricism of Locke could not account for or justify. Hence Kant realized that Empiricism, because it failed to recognize these features in knowledge, was destructive of all science. Science is of the universal and necessary. It professes to establish laws that are true in all cases, in the past, present and future, unless a miracle intervenes. But Empiricism or knowledge grounded on mere sense-experience informs us at best of what has actually taken place in what we or our ancestors have actually observed or tried out by experiment. Since the future cannot be experienced, Empiricism tells us only about some, not about all cases. Hence it fails to establish the genuine universality of any principle or law. Moreover, if according to Locke and the Empiricists the essences of things are unknown and unknowable to the human mind, then of course necessity and universality which in any system of realism, are based on the essences of things, cannot be derived from extramental reality.

Kant saw clearly that mere experience or Empiricism, which informs us only of *what is* or *what was* but never of what is necessary or *must* be, cannot establish the feature of necessity which is an essential characteristic of all science.

The rejection of Empiricism was not the only effect which the diligent study of Hume's destructive criticism wrought in the mind of Kant. A still more far-reaching effect was the upsetting of his confidence in the Leibnitzian development of the Cartesian philosophy, which up to this time, that is, during his pre-critical career, he accepted dogmatically (as "something taught") without question or examination from his masters, — Wolfe and Knutzen. "It was Hume," Kant confesses, "who aroused me from my dogmatic slumber." If Kant slumbered in dogmatism, he now awoke under the influence of Hume, to a new attitude of mind towards knowledge,—criticism. Controlled by this new critical temper of mind, Kant examined the Leibnitzian version of the innatism of Des-

cartes, which he had up to this time acquiescingly adopted
but now found wanting. He realized clearly, that though
innatism could account for the features of universality
and necessity in our knowledge, yet it could not explain
another essential feature of science, namely the continuous additions of new knowledge to our previously acquired
store. Every effort of deductive analysis could at best
only reveal what was already enfolded or implicit in the
innate ideas of Leibnitz. Hence beyond making explicit
what was already implicit in innate ideas, no new knowledge could be acquired.

Kant, then, rejected both English Empiricism and the
Leibnitzian development of Cartesianism, because of
their inadequacy to justify the twofold demands of scientific knowledge, and set about constructing a new philosophy which to his mind would be adequate to explain
both these demands. This new philosophy of Kant professed to be, like Scholasticism, a *"via media"* between the
exaggerated sensism of the English school (Empiricism)
and the exaggerated intellectualism of the Cartesians
(Innatism), but unfortunately Kant derived all the intellectual elements of knowledge not from objective reality
as Scholasticism does, but from out the mind itself, thereby making it impossible for the human mind to know any
reality (the-thing-in-itself) outside and independent of
the mind. An exposition and criticism of the peculiar
philosophy of Kant will be set forth in its proper place.

What interests us now is, that since Kant's philosophy
in its development was the outcome of a critical investigation of Cartesianism and Empiricism, Kantianism is a
fitting climax to our study of the two former systems,
and should naturally be included in the English school.

There is still a more intimate and racial reason for
including Kant in the English School. Hume was Scotch
and Kant was of Scotch extraction. It is natural to suppose, then, that Kant was attracted to Hume by a peculiar
sympathy on account of the common bond of race that
existed between them. There is no doubt that Hume exercised more influence over Kant than did any other phil-

osopher.   It is Hume that inspired Kant to adopt towards
knowledge the attitude of criticism.   For these reasons
also we may justly conclude that Kant belongs to the
English School.   We shall include therefore, in the history of Modern English thought an exposition and criticism of the Kantian philosophy.

CHAPTER I

LIFE AND TIMES

John Locke (1632-1704)

THE careers of Locke, Berkeley, and Hume were contemporaneous with the years of the Colonial period of America, and, we may add, with the dark days of the penal laws in Great Britain and Ireland. Locke was born twelve years after the landing of the Mayflower; Hume died (1776) the year we proclaimed our independence; Berkeley in 1753.

Locke and Berkeley had closer interests and contacts with Colonial America than those which arise from a common language and common traditions. Locke was not only a philosopher but a prolific political writer. At the invitation of Lord Ashley, one of the most influential proprietors in Carolina, Locke drew up "A Fundamental Constitution for the Government of Carolina." The influence of his political writings helped, no doubt, to mould the principles of the Declaration of Independence. At one time Locke seriously intended coming to America for the benefit of his health. Berkeley actually lived here for three years, and wrote some of his most charming works on the cool shores of the now fashionable Newport, Rhode Island.

Great Britain and Ireland, then, through their trinity of thinkers exerted considerable influence upon American thought. There are striking affinities between Berkeley's Idealism and Mrs. Eddy's so-called Christian Science. The graceful expression of pragmatical William James — "a stream of consciousness," which purports to be a description of human personality, is thoroughly Humean. America is the melting pot of all the leading European influences. As the typical American will some day arise as an amalgam of all the leading strains of character in Europe, so the national thought of America is today, and bids fair to be in the future, some kind of an elective synthesis of the ever changing thought systems of Europe, spoken of course with an American accent, that is, made acceptable to American tastes by a pinch of piquancy contributed by our native genius. American philosophy is only the echo of French, English, and German philosophies. Our mental radio is always set to pick up the prevailing thought of Europe.

Of course, we are now speaking of non-Catholic thought. This non-Catholic thought is ever seething and boiling like the witches' cauldron in Macbeth. It is liquid in its movements; its ingredients are never the same; it is marked by change upon change. "No finality" is its sceptical watchword. Some new assumption or unproved hypothesis is advanced by some leading scientist, or some new principle is erected into an unproved dogma by some distinguished philosopher. A host of worshippers, eager for something new, rather than for something true, pay homage to the most recent intellectually constructed idol. Then the philosophers step in. Forgetful of exercising their critical reflection to decide whether the new theory or principle is really established as true and certain, they seem rather to be spellbound by an ecstatic admiration for the new "idol of the tribe." Thus, captivated by the vision of giving to the world a new system of philosophy, they gamble on the risk of interpreting anew all reality in the light, or in the darkness, of the new but doubtful or false hypothesis or principle. Thus the new system, however logically it may be constructed, will partake of the doubt or falsehood of its ultimate premise. What a host of philosophical substitutes for the soul, for God, for Christianity are now being born from the doubtful or false implications of complete evolution? What a multiplicity of philosophies sprang up, not to mention his other doctrines, from the unproved assumption of Descartes, that the direct and immediate object of knowledge is not something outside and independent of the mind, but something within the mind, something subjective or psychical! Locke without examination or criticism adopted this same principle. And from this principle, united with another false hypothesis, that the only source of human knowledge is sense *experience*, a principle that implies that the supersensible or metempirical is *unknown*, what a brood of "isms" were popularized not only in England, but in France and Germany, all claiming the maternal womb of Empiricism as their origin!

Who, then was Locke? John Locke was born in Somersetshire, near Bristol, the same year as the Jewish-Dutch Pantheist, Spinoza, 1632. His father was a country lawyer, who at the time of the Puritan revolt, became a petty officer in the army of the notorious Cromwell. Like Descartes he lost his mother while he was yet very young.

He was well educated, entering Westminster School at the age of 14, and afterwards Christ Church, Oxford, where he received his degree of Bachelor and Master of Arts, 1658. At the beginning of his college career, theological studies and the ministry attracted him. Those he soon relinquished to dabble in the study of medicine and chemistry. At the age of forty-two (1674), he obtained, strange to say, not the degree of M.D. but that of Bachelor of Medicine. He never practiced publicly his profession, though he was a private physician to more than one nobleman of his time, and went by the appellation of "Doctor." He never married. When urged to do so, he playfully replied that "his health was the only mistress he had for a long time courted — a mistress so reserved," he added, "that it would likely require all that remained of his life to secure her good graces, and keep her in good humor." His health was never very robust.

In the capacity of Secretary to several English noblemen, he visited and lived for some time in France and Germany. During the troublous times in which Locke lived, Holland became the favorite refuge for political exiles.

A political suspect, he lived in Holland for over five years where he became a favorite of William of Orange, and assisted him in preparing the revolution that placed William on the English throne. His sympathies were, therefore, dashed with splashes of "orange." Besides the aforementioned "Constitution of Carolina," Locke wrote many other political works. For his time, he was liberal in his politics and leaned towards democracy. In his "Essay on Toleration" he was at least broad-minded enough to extend liberty of conscience to the Protestant species of the human race, but classing Catholics with Atheists, excluded both from all political privileges. His most considerable political work was "Two Treatises on Government" (1670). This work based the origin of society on the non-Catholic "Contract theory" afterwards popularized by Rousseau, opposed absolute monarchy, and acknowledged that the people were the sole origin of all government. Sixty-eight years before Locke, the well known Spanish Jesuit, Suarez, had given expression, in his "Defence of the Faith," written against the autocratic claims of James I of England, to the traditional Catholic doctrine that civil government has its rightful origin in the "consent of the governed" though his explanation of that "consent" is essentially different from that of Locke.

If the "reds" today picked up Locke's "Treatise on Government" they could gloat over the curious doctrine contained therein, that the *right of property* is exclusively based on *labor.*

A tiny book, perhaps one of the most charming works that came from Locke's pen, the reading of which any teacher would enjoy, is his "Thoughts Concerning Education." Locke insists, and he is right, that the crowning success of a college education does not consist in the amount of knowledge which teachers may have succeeded in drumming into the heads of students, but rather in a taste for and a habit of study, which the power of a good teacher succeeds in inspiring in a student. The bloom and fruit of a true education develops, not so much while the student is in school or college, but when he leaves it. A *habit of study* that endures for life is the real test of an education. Locke expresses this truth in the following passage, from his "Essay on Education." "The main point," he says, "to teach the child is to get a mastery over his inclinations and submit his appetite to reason." "The

teacher" he says, "should remember that his or her
business is not so much to teach (the pupil) all that is
knowable, as to raise in him a love and esteem of knowledge, and put him in the right way of knowing and im-
proving himself when he has a mind to it." To Locke's
earnest advocacy of bodily exercise as a part of liberal
education may be traced the popularity of athletics in the
colleges of the English speaking world.

The work, however, which interests us most at present, and with which fame has associated the name of
Locke, is his "Essay Concerning the Human Understanding." The first edition of this "Essay" appeared in 1690,
when Locke was fifty-eight years of age. It is this philosophical work which will be the subject of our exposition
and criticism. Locke's influence was immense. As he himself confessed that he owed his philosophical awakening
to the study of Descartes, so French thought from Condillac to Bergson was afterwards deeply influenced by
Locke. Locke died in 1704, having lived two years over
the scriptural span of life for man, of three score and
ten. One of his biographers describing his death says:
"On October 28, 1704, while sitting on his chair in his
room where Lady Masham, his lifelong friend, had cheered
him by reading from the Psalms of David, death came
upon him without a struggle, as sleep upon a child." In
his religious views Locke embraced "Liberalism." In fact
he stands out as one of the founders of "modern liberalism" in religion. He looked upon Christianity, not as a
positive religion of definite dogmas and precepts, but as
a religion of human kindness and love without any definite creed, or definite form of worship. Locke was more
of a Deist than a Christian. The Bishops of the Established Church of England did not look upon Locke, the
Freethinker, with friendly favor. His controversy with
Stillingfleet, Bishop of Worcester, bears witness to the
bitter opposition of the Church of England towards Locke.

Before entering into the study of Locke's philosophy,
it will be well to direct your attention to certain mental
peculiarities of the Protestant mind of England, of which

John Locke was a typical embodiment. Indeed, as we shall proceed in our study of non-Catholic thought we shall discover that Protestantism seems to have given an abnormal twist to the mentality of its adherents, which precludes it from arriving at those vital truths which are of the highest moment to humanity. The characteristic which I wish to insist upon is, strange to say, a distrust of the *God-given gift of natural reason and a contempt for logical sequence.* That Locke sorely lacked the logical instinct, allow me to corroborate by quoting the judgment of a competent critic. Professor Morris, late of Johns Hopkins, and the translator from German into English of Ueberweg's "History of Philosophy," gives this judgment of Locke: "Locke's very desire," he says, "for plainness and intelligibility has rendered his style, by universal admission, loose and inexact, not to mention the 'colorless prolixity' in him, and in most English philosophical writers, and has consequently made his reasoning obscure and his conclusions uncertain." (British Thought and Thinkers, p. 180.)

Locke himself is honest about the matter, and expressly boasts of his scorn and contempt for scientific logic. Cleverly satirical, were it only true, is the following passage: "God has not been so sparing to men," says Locke, "to make them barely two-legged creatures and left it to Aristotle to make them rational; that is, those few of them that he could get to examine the grounds of the syllogism."[1] Thus did he attempt by ridicule as superficial as his logic to defend his own inconsequences, by endeavoring to change into contempt the world's admiration for the giantlike mentality of the Stagirite. But as Belfort Bax says, "Locke was an Englishman of Englishmen, alike in character and writings. There is in him the common sense force of the English character, and all its lack of subtility, and we may add all its honest contempt for the qualities it does not itself possess."[2] If a man can become an expert in thinking, without studying the

---

[1]"Essay", B IV, C XVII, 4.
[2]History of Philosophy, p. 188.

science of logical reasoning, as Locke maintains, why, it may be retorted, should not the common sense of mankind permit a man to practice medicine without studying the principles of medicine, or practice law without studying the principles of justice and jurisprudence? Or has worldly wisdom come to this pass, that it jealously demands expert knowledge to protect our temporal interests, while any ninny amateur is quite competent to guide our steps in the attainment of our eternal destiny? Because Edison was a great mechanical inventor, was he therefore a great philosopher? Because Sir Oliver Lodge is undoubtedly an authority on Physics, is he therefore to be accepted as a modern prophet of a new Revelation, and a preacher of a new Ether-God? Now even if we grant, with competent observers, that the English mind is proverbially indifferent to the cultivation of logical acumen, this indifference cannot be entirely attributed to any want of native genius. The real cause of this strange deficiency in accurate reasoning lies deeper. It is to be found in the overwhelming influences which the *attitude of Protestantism towards natural reason* has exerted upon the national thought, not only in England, but over all of those countries wherein it has obtained a dominant sway. The witty, satirical remark of Locke regarding Aristotle, as the recognized teacher of the world of the science of logical reasoning, was only the echo of the contempt of Luther and the early reformers for the God-given gift of natural reason in man. And this distrustful contempt of the ability of human reason to arrive at the knowledge of those supersensible truths most vital for humanity, the existence of God, the existence and immortality of the soul, and of the freedom of the human will, has persisted in the temper of Protestant philosophies to the present day. Strange as it may appear, the Catholic church has always been the defender and champion of human reason, while Protestantism discredits, if it does not altogether deny, its validity. Because as Ueberweg says, "In the first heat of the conflict the Reformers regarded the head of the Catholic church as Antichrist, and Aristotle, the chief of Scholasticism, as the godless bulwark of the Papists."[1] Hence we hear Luther in his well known uncouth diction railing against natural reason, and logic, as incompetent to attain knowledge of even the first principles of morality and religion. Luther says: "Man's reason is, perhaps, adequate for knowing how to build houses, make clothes, marry, fight, navigate, — but in things concerning God, to know how to act in this respect, human nature is altogether dense, dull, and blind, and cannot show even so much as a hair's breadth of what these things are. Presumptuous enough, indeed, she (reason) is to go floundering and blundering in, like a blind horse. But all that she has to say on the subject is certainly false and erroneous."[2] No wonder Protestantism later on developed into Agnosticism, which, as we go on in our study, we shall see is the logical outcome of the principles of the English school of philosophy.

It is interesting to infer from this quotation that Luther and nascent Protestantism were Empiricistic, that is, denied to reason the power of knowing the supersensible, a century and a half before that system was popularized by Locke and his disciples. Consequently Lutheranism was Agnostic almost three centuries before Huxley invented the charming name of "Agnosticism" to dignify in English thought the tragic death of human reason. Kant also, whom Paulsen calls the philosopher of Protestantism, did not hesitate to say, "I destroyed reason to make room for faith." He did not realize that he thus made faith irrational. Jansen points out in the following passage the hatred which the original reformers openly manifested towards reason and logic. Jansen says: "Luther had denounced the universities as dens of murderers, temples of Moloch, synagogues of corruption. In a sermon preached in the year 1521, of which several editions were published, he had actually gone so far as to say that the universities were only worthy of being reduced to dust, and that nothing more hellish or devilish

---

[1]History of Philosophy, Vol. II, p. 15.
[2]History of the German People, Jansen, Vol. XIC, p. 120.

had ever appeared on the face of the earth from the beginning of things or ever could appear."[1] In his passionate hatred, Luther went so far as to characterize reason as "the prostitute of Satan."

Why is it that Luther was an implacable enemy of natural reason? Dollinger, cited by Jansen[2] gives the following reason.

"The reason why Luther was so fiercely opposed to human reason and to the study of philosophy is easily explained by the fact that he had a distinct feeling, and a certain intuitive sense, that his doctrine on God as the author of sin, and of man as naturally unfree, was condemned by philosophy as the most arrant falsehood."

"So long," says Moehler,[3] "as the teaching of Luther and Calvin was believed to be true, there was no poetry, no history, no philosophy in the Protestant Church. It was, indeed, a positive fact, that so long as the Protestant community remained Lutheran, it had no philosophy, and when it acquired a system of philosophy, it was no longer Lutheran. Such is the way their faith flies from philosophy and their philosophy from faith."

Melanchthon also said, in a pamphlet against Enser in the year 1521, "Never had anything more corrupt or godless been invented than universities. . . Not Popes, but the devil himself was their originator. Wycliffe had been the first to recognize that the universities were schools of Satan. Could he have said anything more wise and godly? The Jews offered up youths to Moloch. And at the universities young men were offered up to pagan idols. A man who boasts of the title of philosopher cannot be called a Christian."[4] Protestant thought was never afraid of riches, empire, and political power. These it flatters and worships. One thing it instinctively feared in its inception and development — namely, the calm, clear eye of reason. Hence the frantic efforts of its philosophy to

---

[1]History of the German People, Vol. III, p. 355.
[2]Vol. XIV, p. 123.
[3]Jansen, V-XIV, p. 125 (cited).
[4]History of the German People, Vol. III, p. 355.

convince the intellectual world that natural reason cannot
be trusted in any of its conclusions which give us a knowledge of the supersensible. Though in principle the distrust of reason began with Luther and the early Reformers, yet we find this same distrust reechoed by the
leaders of Puritanical Calvinism in our own land over rock-
ribbed New England. Cotton Mather (1663-1728) manifested this same contempt of reason in the following
passage from his "Student and Preacher" addressed in
early days to the men of Harvard and Yale. He says:
"Hearken ye men of Harvard and Yale College to old
Eubulus, exhorting you with his counsel. In most academies of this world nothing is acquired but worldly wisdom; the philosophy taught in them is not philosophy but
foolosophy. Listen not to that smoke-selling chandler,
the muddy-headed pagan, Aristotle, to whose yoke souls
called rational have submitted their necks and written
prodigious cartloads of stuff to explain the Peripatetic
philosophy————. The vulgar logic, instead of leading
the mind into truth, merely enables one to carry on alter-
cations and logomacies, to exhibit in the pompous forms
of art, with trifling application and illustration, what
every one does by nature and custom————. What I say
of logic I say of metaphysics, which a learned man too
justly called *disciplinarum omnium excrementum*. Over
Ethics the academies spend too much time, plough too
long — it is all over a sham————. Tired with academic
futilities, betake yourself to that best school of Mosaic
philosophy; read the 'Philosophia Vetus ac Vera' of the
rare Dickinson, rather than the hypothesis of the inquisi-
tive sons of the wild ass's colt. Avoid philosophical ro-
mances and get as thorough an insight as you can into
the principles of our perpetual dictator, Sir Isaac Newton.
I hope it will be no indecency in me to say that if you
desire to see the largest collection of the discoveries which
the last age has made in philosophy adapted into the
general capacity of the reader, you have this prepared in
a book entitled the *Christian Philosopher*."[1]

[1] Woodbridge Riley, American Philosophy, p. 195.

These few testimonies, which could be multiplied by the hundreds, will give some idea of the scorn and contempt with which human reason was viewed by the religion of "Protest" in its inception. This distrust of reason was of course a logical inference of the doctrine of the "total depravity" of human nature as a consequence of original sin, adopted by the early reformers. Every action of totally depraved man was sinful, and every conclusion of reason that professed to know anything of God or man's ultimate destiny was worthless.

But no religion can long endure without some basic philosophy. The adherents of any religion are rational beings, and they will naturally exercise their reason on the most vital problems of life. Hence as soon as the Protestant revolt became an established fact, the philosophers of the many sectarian creeds, which were the offspring of Protestantism, proceeded forthwith to harmonize their doctrines with the claims of reason, and thus set up as many contradictory philosophies as there were contradictory creeds. And since the one principle in which the religionists of "protest" were all agreed was "private judgment," a principle which assumes that the source and norm of all truth are the judgments which each man thinks are true, private judgment became the measure by which divine revelation was adjudged. This, of course, is Rationalism. The authority of man's word superseded the authority of God's word as manifested by the divinely established Church. Hence the philosophy of pure Rationalism or Free Thought was set up as the Supreme Court of final appeal in the religion of Protestantism.

This rationalistic spirit, though logically the outcome of private judgment, acquired a new strength as an exaggerated, though natural reaction, against the blind faith of Luther and his irrational contempt of reason in all things religious. A brief account of the developments of Rationalism in the history of non-Catholic religious thought is interesting.

Its first offspring was Calvinism or Puritanism. This repellent creed did indeed believe in the Holy Trinity, but God the Father of Puritanism was not God the Father of Catholicity. To the Puritan, God was the direct author of sin: He foreordains men to commit sin that He may then justly punish them. The Puritan believed in the divinity of Christ, in the Incarnation, and the Redemption, yet the Christ of the Puritan Fathers was not the Christ of the Fathers of the Catholic Church. To the Catholic, Christ died for all men and wishes all to be saved; to the Puritan, Christ died only for the select few, and so far was Puritanism from teaching that the merits of the redemption extended to all, that it held the rather odious doctrine that the vast majority of the human race was foreordained, no matter what they might do in life, to eternal perdition pointedly illustrating the facetious old rhyme—

> "Men can and men can't,
> Men would and men won't,
> They're damned if they do,
> And they're damned if they don't."

This ferocious creed Michael Wigglesworth of Malden fame gave undisguised utterance to in his uncouth and sulphureous poem (1669), "The Day of Doom," that stands in New England literature as a grim monument to the capricious tyranny of the deity of Puritanism without a counterpart in any other literature of the world.

The Puritan conception of man was no less degrading. Human nature was believed to be totally depraved; man was not by nature a moral being; freedom of will was denied him; he was an intellectual beast, the monster of creation, the plaything of dire necessity, who could grovel in his evil passions unto sin, but not head against them unto virtue. If it is hard for consistent thinking to understand the exalted virtue which has ever been associated with the Puritan name, it is even more difficult to comprehend how a people who denied to man the noble prerogative of individual freedom could have appropriated to themselves the unique honor of becoming for the human race the champions of political liberty.

Horace Mann said in bitterness of Puritanism, that "it taught not the existence of a God worthy to be loved, nor a type of man, it may be added, worthy to be admired." And Moses Coit Tyler in his "American Literature" says of it: "No pagan of antiquity, no heretic of the ages, no philosophical system of history has ever attributed to the divine Being a character more execrable and loathsome than did Puritanism." This first fashion of Rationalistic religion passed away. "As a system of thought, Puritanism has had its day. Intellectually, Calvinism is dead. No philosophical writer of the present day ever thinks of the answer it once gave to the awful riddle of the universe." (Joseph Henry Allen).

In the eighteenth century a new fashion of thoroughly rationalistic thought took the place of the Puritanism of the seventeenth. It was the complete reversal of the position of Lutheranism. Luther and his followers proclaimed that reason could know nothing of God; the Deists, that reason alone could know whatever there is to be known of God.

The Deist accosted the bewildered Puritan and said, "You have attempted to interpret your Bible by the light of your own individual reason; you have gathered from it an ideal of God that is monstrous and a conception of man that is degrading. Abandon the Bible of Revelation, which you have evidently misunderstood, and substitute for it as the only source of truth, *the works of God in nature*. Shut out the voice of heaven; place all your sufficiency in human reason; hearken to the voice of nature; 'find sermons in stones and good in everything.' With the Englishman Collins trust not in prophecy, with Woolston believe not in miracles, with Tindal deny revelation, with Morgan abandon the Old Testament, and with Chubb inveigh against Christian morality. Take up the pick of the geologist, the scalpel of the anatomist, the test tube of the chemist, the telescope of the astronomer; draw the lightning from the clouds; study the natural sciences and whatever knowledge you may glean from their data about God and the soul; let that be your religion." Such in brief is Deism. Deism was essentially a retrograde movement. It would not only deprive Hebrew history of the light of revelation that kept shining in the midst of an idolatrous and darkened world, the knowledge of the true God, but would extinguish from the pages of modern history as a myth, the pure white light of the Christian faith, to which we owe all western civilization. You see, then, what Deism is, nothing short of a *refined paganism*.

Deism did indeed admit a personal God as the cause of the universe. But once having created the world, once having set in motion the forces which we call the laws of nature, as a watchmaker would construct and adjust and set moving the wheels of a watch, then did the Deists conceive of their Deity as living apart from His own creation, permitting it to wag as it would without care for, or interference with, its activities. To the Deist no special Providence of God could possibly find a place to suspend or change the rigid mechanism of nature's laws that grind out the grist of your life and mine. Prayer would be unavailing, because the Deist's deity has no concern for his creatures. The miracles of Lourdes today would, according to deistic principles, be an impossibility, because to a deist the laws of nature are inexorably fixed. If the God of Puritanism was tyrannically cruel, the God of Deism was as indifferent and implacable as an absentee landlord. Like Puritanical Calvinism, Deism became obsolete. In the nineteenth century, owing to the influence of Locke, Hume, and especially of Kant, natural reason was again declared incapable of reaching any knowledge of God's existence. The deistic form of Rationalism was discredited, and another new fashion of thought, which is known as *Agnosticism*, dominated the non-Catholic world during the nineteenth century. Those seesawing systems which move up and down upon the pivot of Rationalism without the slightest effort to show that divine revelation is reasonable, modern thought calls progress. Whereas the truth is that the ineptitude of reason in the field of

Natural Theology proclaimed by Luther, and which two centuries of Protestant thought instinctively accepted, became once more a dogma of Kantian Agnosticism.

Towards the end of the nineteenth, and during the first quarter of the present century a new way of knowledge to reach God, a way that is entirely independent of reason, was invented. Man is to be permitted to retain his prerogative of being a rational animal in the field of material sciences, but for the attainment of truths most vital to humanity, men are to be shorn of their reason and transformed into *sentimental, feeling,* blindly voluntaristic animals. No longer may man *know* God on rational grounds. If he is to reach or rather grope for God at all, he must do so by instinct, sentiment, feeling, blindly impelling man to *will* God, not to know him. Such has been the doctrine of Modernism.

This last verdict of modern thought on man's nature proclaims man to be *rational* so long as he confines the exercise of reason to temporal and material concerns, but to be a *mere animal* led by instinct and feeling in all matters that concern God and his attributes. One would naturally think that the noblest faculty of man, his reason, should be brought into play to reach the highest and noblest object — God, and if we must have it, that his lowest, blind propensities be brought into requisition to reach the lower and less noble objects — material concerns. But such is the topsy-turvyism of modern thought.

Nor is this sentimental, voluntaristic approach to God the last development of Rationalistic Protestant thought. Its very latest vagary is so esoteric, so difficult to understand, so violently opposed to the common sense of men, that we shall express it in the words of one of its votaries. It is supposed to be the newest concept of God that is based upon the assumed hypothesis of Evolution. Prof. Alexander (Manchester University, England) says: "God, as actually possessing deity, does not exist, but as an ideal is always *becoming*; but God as the whole universe tending towards deity does exist." "As an actual existent, God is the infinite world with its nisus towards deity."

(Quoted by Dr. Sheen, "God and Intelligence," p. 54.)
The actually existing God is, then, identical with the universe; and this *actual*, ever-evolving God is gradually producing the deity who is not yet completed, but who is "becoming," but shall never arrive.

The facile complacency with which non-Catholic thought changes from age to age its ever varying positions without the slightest apology for its former admitted errors points to only one conclusion, that non-Catholic thought has never been, and is not today, certain of the truth of its professed teachings. It was sceptical in the beginning, and it is sceptical today. If the knowledge of truth is a discovery and not a human creation, then private judgment, with its varied and contradictory findings, can never grasp any permanent, consistent truth that is independent of individual minds. If we are justified in judging the future by the past, is it not a fair surmise that the present religion of the God of "becoming" will again be discredited by the chameleon philosophers of the next generation, and some other new, ephemeral divinity and religion become the fashion? No respectable person wishes to appear wholly irreligious. He must have some religion, not one so objectively true and certain as to demand from him the supreme sacrifice of his life, but a religion that will be at least a kind of perfumed opinion to sprinkle on Sundays over his person.

CHAPTER II

PHILOSOPHICAL SYSTEM

John Locke (1632-1704)

THE study of traditional Scholasticism as a system and a method lingered on in Oxford for many years after the so-called Reformation. It is true that in Locke's day the pristine vigor of Scholasticism outside of Spain[1] had deteriorated. In England the tradition of genuine Scholasticism was vitiated by the prevailing Nominalism of Occam. In Italy the ancient pagan systems revived and popularized by the Renaissance weakened it. In France the rise of Cartesianism tended to supersede it. The spirit of the Reformation was naturally opposed to the philosophy of the Catholic Church.

Hence, as time went on it was to be expected that an irreconcilable incompatibility of temperament should arise in the household of the Reformation between the fair and favored daughter of Catholicism — genuine Scholasticism — and her uncongenial mate, Protestantism. An absolute divorce between them was the inevitable result. And so it came to pass. During the three centuries that have elapsed since Descartes attempted to supersede Scholasticism, how numerous are the systems of philosophy that in their day were accepted because new, and have since been rejected because adjudged untrue? Indeed, as we saw in the preceding chapter, Protestantism began by summarily ejecting from its home all philosophy, and it has not, even to the present day, found any system of rational thought with which it is willing to live, even for any considerable time, in peace and amity.

Locke, during his university career, conceived a deep aversion for Scholasticism. Its exact, intellectual definitions, its rigid, logical sequences did not appeal to a mentality which professed to limit the sphere of knowledge

---

[1]Suarez died fifteen years before Locke was born.

to the low level of the things of sense, and which, to grasp, demanded no higher faculty than the imagination. This professed philosophy of Sensism, which Locke popularized, because shallow, and easily read by other amateurish and uncritical gentlemen, gained the reputation of apparent clearness and intelligibility.

If we are to credit contemporary authorities, both the scholarship and discipline of Oxford during the first half of the eighteenth century, and *for many years before*, had reached a low ebb. Gibbon regarded his residence there as the "most idle and unprofitable period of his life." Adam Smith, who lived in Oxford from 1740 to 1747, observes:—"In the University of Oxford the greater part of the professors have, *for many years*, given up even the pretence of teaching. The discipline is, in general, contrived not for the benefit of the students, but for the ease of the masters. As for the undergraduates, they wasted their time in drinking and gambling."[1]

Locke was a self-made philosopher. He read, no doubt, all the systems of his day that fell into his hands. But he seems to have been a man of moods — moods engendered by the suggestions of the last philosophical writer whom he read and consulted. Hence the conclusions he arrived at while dominated by one mood, contradicted the results of his thinking while under the influence of another mood. As a typical Englishman, Locke seems oblivious of the necessity of logically harmonizing what he wrote at one time with what he wrote at another time. Hence his "Essay," the construction of which extended over many years, is teeming with contradictions and inconsistencies. Deeply influenced by Descartes and the Cartesians, Locke's philosophy seems to be an eclectic medley of many of the systems that eventually developed from Cartesian principles. Traditionally Locke is characterized as a Sensist; but many passages from his "Essay" may be cited to show that he was also an "intellectualist." Berkeley, who was an ardent student of Locke, could see

[1]Life of John Wesley by Frank Banfield, Westminster Biographies.

him only as an Idealist, while Locke himself professed Realism. It is quite possible to quote passages from his works to establish that, at times, he seems to advocate Occasionalism. No wonder, then, that the canny Scotchman Hume reduced Locke's confused medley of systems to universal scepticism.

It is obviously difficult, therefore, to set forth a consistent exposition of Locke's system. We shall endeavor, however, to enumerate the chief characteristics of Locke's philosophy, and in each case indicate the fatal consequences that are logically implicit in them, and which have actually been developed by the successors of his school.

Locke begins his famous "Essay" by repudiating and refuting innate ideas and therefore innate principles. The mind originally is, then, according to Locke, a "tabula rasa" or clean slate void of all ideas. Before entering, however, into his main inquiry, which was how ideas came to be written in the mind, Locke dogmatically assumed without examination or criticism the well-known idealistic postulate of Descartes, namely, that the direct and immediate objects that terminate his knowledge are not any realities or actually existing objects outside and independent of the mind, but objects lying wholly within the mind, that is, his own "ideas;" objects, therefore, mental or psychical. The world of direct and immediate knowledge is, therefore, not without but within him.

Immediately connected with this restriction of what we first and foremost know is the slipshod, vague meaning which Locke attached to the word "idea," a meaning that has been perpetuated by English psychological and pedagogical writers ever since, engendering in English thought the fatal tendency of refusing to distinguish clearly between the spiritual faculty of intellect, and the materially dependent faculties of the senses. This tendency to confuse intellectual with sensuous knowledge is the characteristic weakness of English thought. Both the idealistic principle and this confused meaning of "idea" are expressed by Locke in the following passages:—

"This much I thought necessary to say concerning the occasion of this inquiry into *human understanding*. But before I proceed on to what I have thought on this subject, I must here, in the entrance, beg pardon of my reader for the frequent use of the word "idea," which he will find in the following treatise, it being that term, which I think, serves best to stand for *whatsoever is the object of the understanding, when a man thinks*. I have used it to express whatever is meant *by phantasm, notion, species,* or whatever it is which the mind can be employed about in thinking: and I could not avoid frequently using it." (Essay, Introd., 8.)

Again he says:—"The mind hath no other immediate object but its own ideas which it alone does or can contemplate." (B IV, I, 1.)

Two unproved assertions are dogmatically stated in these passages. *First*, that an "idea" stands for whatever is an object of knowledge. Since, then, an "idea" is always a mental object, it follows from this statement that the objects which we first of all and directly fix our gaze upon are never any existent realities that are extramental, but realities that are wholly within the mind, intramental. *Secondly*, the term "idea," which in Scholastic philosophy is reserved to express the purely intellectual representation in the mind of some reality, is here sloppily employed by Locke to designate, not merely as he says, a notion or species as "man," "substance," triangle," which are wholly intellectual because universal, but is also used, with characteristic Lockean indistinctness of thought, to signify a *"phantasm,"* which, because it is always a picture or image of the imagination, is wholly sensuous and singular. It would be just as appropriate to call an ox an angel as to call a "phantasm" an "idea." To call a concept or notion of the intellect, and a phantasm of the imagination, two things so totally different in their natures, by the same term — "idea" — is an indication at the very threshold of his philosophy of Locke's tendency to confound intellect with sense, and to make man a mere glorified animal. So many outstanding philosophers of the ages — Plato, Soc-

rates, Aristotle, Descartes, Leibnitz, and even Kant —
were never guilty of this confusion.

Now what are the logical consequences, in the first
place, of the doctrine which Locke accepted from Descartes, namely, that the objects which the mind directly
and immediately knows are "ideas"?

The fatal consequence is this. If the first and direct
materials of all knowledge presented to the mind are only
"ideas," then that is all the material the mind can ever
know. "Ideas" are the only materials the mind has to
work upon wherewith to construct all its knowledge.
Modern Idealists express this consequence by saying "the
mind can never transcend itself."

What can be constructed from "ideas" but an edifice
of "ideas" no matter how you manipulate them? Suppose there were no other material or commodity on earth
for man to work upon but wood; then all his efforts could
not make anything except out of wood. In like manner,
if as Locke says, the only material of knowledge given to
man, out of which he is to construct all his knowledge,
are "ideas," then out of the material of those ideas he
cannot fashion anything except other "ideas." All his
judgments and reasoning will be confined, like a squirrel
in a cage, within the realm of "ideas." Hence the whole
round of existing things outside the closed circle of
"ideas" — matter, other human beings, soul, God, etc., —
will be forever shut out from the range of his knowledge;
he will be doomed forever to gaze, like a maniac, at his
own "ideas." This is why Locke's philosophy logically
developed at the hands of Berkeley and Hume and their
disciples into certain forms of Idealism. Locke himself
was not an Idealist, though logically he ought to have
been. His sturdy or stubborn common sense saved his
sanity. Yet it is no compliment to his intellectuality to
say, that while he believed in Realism, he implicitly taught
Idealism.

The conclusion, based upon Locke's principles, at
which we have arrived, namely, that he could *know*
nothing except his own "ideas," is corroborated by Locke's

own words. "Since the mind," he says, "in all its thoughts
and reasonings, hath no other immediate object but its
own ideas, which it alone does or can contemplate, it is
evident that our *knowledge* is only conversant about
them." (B IV. C-I-1.) Locke reiterates this principle
when he says:—"All our knowledge consists in the view
the mind has of its own ideas, which is the utmost light
and greatest certainty we with our faculties and in our
way of knowledge are capable of." (IV. II, 1.) These
quotations are clearly decisive in proving that Locke was
logically an Idealist. Hence, he thus explicitly defines
knowledge, and emphasizes his definition by italics:—
"Knowledge, then, seems to me to be nothing but the perception of *the connexion of and agreement, or disagreement and repugnancy of, any of our ideas.* In this alone
it consists." (B IV. C-I-2.) Since, then, every conclusion
of reasoning is derived from premises, which according
to Locke are "conversant about ideas," it follows that
every conclusion of reasoning is also conversant about
"ideas" only. Neither (1) perception, therefore, nor (2)
judgment, nor (3) reasoning, can ever pass beyond the
realm of "ideas."

Yet Locke, swayed, no doubt, by his English common
sense, and by the spontaneous conviction of mankind,
made desperate efforts to demonstrate the existence of
objects outside of him "through the intervention of ideas
(the mind) has of them." (B IV. IV, 3.) Nor is he
oblivious of the difficulty of the problem in the face of his
own definition of knowledge — "the perception of the
agreement or disagreement between his own ideas."
Should he arrive at the conclusion, for instance, that "this
paper on which he is writing *exists*," the predicate "exists" is more than a mere idea. For it asserts that the
paper has a mode of existence outside and independent
of his subjective idea of it. The idea is in his mind, and
the paper as an actual existence stands outside his mind
in its own actual state of existence independently of his
mind and of his idea of the paper. How, then, can Locke
consistently maintain his definition of knowledge, unless

he makes "existence," as Green reminded him, a mere idea. But to make "existence" a mere idea is to fall short of what is meant by "existence."

Locke was not unmindful of this difficulty, and so he fairly and squarely states the time-honored and difficult epistemological problem in the following passage. He says:—"But who knows what these ideas may be? Is there anything so extravagant as the imaginations of men's brains? Where is the head that has no chimeras in it? Or if he be a sober and wise man, what difference will there be, by your (Locke's) rules, between his knowledge and that of the most extravagant fancy in the world? They both have their ideas, and perceive their agreement and disagreement one with another. * * * If it be true, that all knowledge lies only in the perception of the agreement or disagreement of our own ideas, the visions of an enthusiast and the reasonings of a sober man will be equally certain. It is no matter how things are; so a man observes but the agreement of his own imagination, and talk conformably, it is all truth, it is all certainty." (B IV. C. IV-1.) The difficulty of ever knowing objective reality through "ideas" in which all knowledge directly terminates is well taken by Locke, and clearly exposed against his own theory. What is his answer? Through the knowledge of his ideas only he struggles bravely to reach a knowledge of objective reality. Let us study the outcome of all his efforts so to do.

"Our knowledge, therefore," he answers, "is real only so far as there is a *conformity* between our ideas and the reality of things." (B IV. C IV, 3.) In this statement he, with sufficient accuracy, states the Scholastic definition of truth. Then he asks these vital questions: "But what shall be here the criterion? How shall the mind, *when it perceives nothing but its own ideas, know that they agree with things themselves*"? This seems not to want difficulty. (B IV. C IV, 3.)

Locke then endeavors to demonstrate the existence of bodies outside of his ideas by different arguments which are based upon the following principles. Bodies exist out-

side of him because he infers their existence by means of
1. The principle of causality.
2. Because things produce therein (in the mind) those
perceptions (ideas) which by the wisdom and will of the
Maker they are ordained and adapted to.
3. Because ideas are the mental representations of
extramental objects.
4. Because of the "vividness" of external sense perceptions (ideas) compared with faintness and feebleness
of those of memory and imagination.

In the following passage Locke states, in proof of the
existence of bodies, both his argument based on the principle of causality and that derived from "the wisdom and
will of the Maker." He says:—"The first are simple ideas
(i.e., ideas derived from the ordinary exercise of the external senses) which, since the mind, as has been shown,
can by no means make to itself, must necessarily be the
product of things operating upon the mind in a natural
way, and producing therein those perceptions which by
the wisdom and will of the Maker they are ordained and
adapted to." (B IV. IV, 4.)

We are not unmindful that there are many epistemol-
ogists, and among them many Neo-Scholastics who, partially at least admit the idealistic principle, in so far as
they teach that the secondary qualities of bodies (the
formal objects of the external senses) are merely intra-
mental phenomena existing formally in the mind and only
causally in outside objects. Their system is known as
Interpretationism or Reasoned Realism in opposition to
Perceptionism which is the common teaching of Scholasticism. This is not the place, however, to give an exposition of these systems.

The question at present is; Do the above arguments of
Locke, based upon the *passivity* of "ideas of sensation,"
and the application of the principle of causality, and the
"wisdom and will of the Maker," succeed in demonstrating
his professed Realism? We venture to say they do not.

We base the first reason for Locke's failure upon his
own account of the nature of "Cause." When Locke an-

alyzes the "idea of Cause," he comes to the conclusion that it is a mere mental creation, having no objective value, and therefore cannot be employed as a premise from which anything actually existing can, as a conclusion, be logically derived. In other words, Locke could not effectively make use of cause, as he understood it, to construct any bridge by which the mind could travel outward from ideas to actual reality. He says:—"So that whatever is considered by us to conduce or operate to the producing any particular, simple idea, or collection of simple ideas, whether substance or mode, which did not before exist, *hath thereby in our minds* (italics ours) the relation of a cause, and so is denominated by us." (B II, XXVI, 1.) For Locke, then, cause is a consideration of the mind, a mere mental phantom, and consequently objectless. Cause, then, as conceived by Locke, exists only in the mind — "hath thereby in our minds the relation of cause." (Consequently cause, being a mental creation only, and really objectless, could never constitute a bridge to lead the mind outwardly from ideas to extramental realities. Nor could "cause," on the supposition of its being wholly subjective, be attributed to outward objects, and applied to those existing objects as the agents that really *produce* our ideas.

The reference of Locke in his argument to "the wisdom and will of the Maker" is obviously an obscure reference to the topsy-turvy proof of Descartes to establish the existence of matter, by making the "wisdom" or veracity of God the means of transition or bridge between the "idea" of matter in the mind to the actual existence of matter outside the mind. But as Descartes failed to demonstrate the objective existence of God from the mere idea of God, so Locke, in repeating the same argument, is doomed to the same fate.

Furthermore, Locke in the above quoted proof assumes the inherent activity of matter. For he implies that matter external to the mind is the cause that "produces" his intramental "simple ideas, or collection of simple ideas." This assumption he expresses in several other passages;

for example, he says:—"For, since there appears not to be any ideas in the mind before the senses have conveyed any in, I conceive the ideas in the understanding are coeval with *sensation; which is such an impression or motion made in some part of the body, as produces some perception* (idea) *in the understanding.*" (B II—I, 23.) (Material bodies, then, *produce* sensation or bodily impressions, and sensation in turn produces ideas in the understanding.)

Yet strange to say, Locke, while under the influence of one of his passing moods, engendered evidently by his approving Descartes' doctrine of the *inertness* of matter, is inclined to deny all activity to matter, and to accept the "exaggerated dualism" and Occasionalism of the Cartesians. For he writes:—"Power * * * is twofold, viz., as able to make, or able to receive, any change. The one may be called *active* and the other *passive* power. Whether matter may be not wholly destitute of active power, as its Author, God, is truly above all passive power, and whether the intermediate state of created spirits be not that alone which is capable of both active and passive power, may be worth consideration." (B II—XXI, 2.) (If it is an open question, then, that matter is void of all activity, as Locke was prone to think when he wrote the above passage, his argument based on the principle of causality to demonstrate the extramental existence of matter falls away) If matter is not active, it cannot be a cause. But Locke's answer — "yes" today and "no" tomorrow to the question, is matter active and consequently a cause? — is another example of his inconsistencies. Locke ridiculed logical consistency. He is therefore consistent with his glorious principle of inconsistency.

The third argument of Locke to demonstrate the existence of bodies is based on the theory of "Representative Perception." (That is, he professes to know objects not directly in themselves, but "through the intervention of ideas.") Ideas, which are the direct and immediate objects of his knowledge, are the intermediaries between the mind and the external object. It is assumed that the intervening ideas are *representations* or *images* of the ex-tramental objects. [Locke argues that since the repre-sentative ideas are known *directly*, then the objects which they image forth or represent are known *indirectly*.]

But it may be asked, how could Locke legitimately plead that his ideas, on the assumption that they alone are directly perceived, are yet representative of existing objects outside themselves? For, how could he ever know that any idea is the image or representation of anything beyond itself, unless he previously knows directly the ex-isting object that idea or image represents? But to know directly such an object would be to abandon "representa-tive perception" and surrender to "direct perceptionism," which Locke has explicitly repudiated. "The mind," he says, "has no other objects but its own ideas."

Besides, to *"re-present"* means to present anew or once more. How could he know that an actually existing object is presented once more to the mind unless he was directly aware of that object at its first or previous presentation?

The last argument to demonstrate the existence of bodies Locke bases upon the "vividness" of the ideas de-rived through the external senses when compared with the languid paleness of ideas of mere imagination and memory. Locke states the argument thus:—"There can be nothing more certain than that the idea we receive from an external object is in our minds. This is intui-tive knowledge. But whether there be anything more than barely that idea in our minds, whether we can thence certainly infer the existence of anything without us, which corresponds to that idea, is that whereof some men[1] think there may be a question made; because men may have such "ideas" in their minds, when no such thing exists, and no such object affects their senses. But yet here, I think, we are provided with an evidence that puts us past doubting. For I ask anyone, whether he be not invincibly conscious to himself of a different perception

------

[1] Descartes and Malebranche.

(idea) when he looks at the sun by day, and thinks of it by night; when he actually tastes wormwood, or smells a rose, or only thinks of that savour or odour? We as plainly find the difference there is between any ideas revived in our minds by our own memory and actually coming into our minds by our senses, as we do between any two distinct ideas." (B IV—II, 14.)

This passage is interesting. Analyzing it, we find that Locke in the first place "begs the question," that is, in the very statement of the question he naively assumes what he professes to demonstrate. He says:—"There can be nothing more certain than that the idea we receive from an external object is in our minds. This is intuitive knowledge." Of course "there can be nothing more certain" than that the *idea as an idea* "is in our minds." That is an intuition of consciousness. But in stating that obvious fact, he avoids the demonstration of the problem which he previously proposed, viz., "How shall the mind, when it perceives nothing but its own ideas, know that they agree with things"?, and with the effrontery of a mendicant boldly "begs that question" by assuming without proof that "we receive our ideas from external objects." If he knows intuitively nothing but his own ideas, how can he assert in the same breath that he knows more than that, namely, that his ideas are produced by external objects?

In the second place, Locke in the above passage covertly flirts with "direct perception," and thereby, implicitly at least, surrenders his theory of "Representationism." But to state explicitly "perceptionism" in the seventeenth century, dominated as it was by the "Representationism" of the Cartesians and the Subjectivism of Protestantism, would be a reversion to discredited Scholasticism. Yet it does seem obvious that in the passage just quoted, wherein Locke endeavors to prove the genuine objectivity of his ideas on the basis of the "vividness" of "ideas of sensation," he, in contradiction to his principle, that he "knows nothing but his own ideas," im-

plicitly admits the "direct perception" of objects outside
of him.

For in that same passage he poses the question:—
"For I ask anyone whether he be not invincibly conscious
to himself of a different perception when *he looks on the*
sun by day, and thinks of it by night; when he *actually*
tastes wormwood, or *smells a rose,* or only thinks of that
savour or odour"? What do the expressions—"looks on
the sun by day," "actually tastes wormwood," "smells a
rose"—plainly mean except the direct perception of those
objects? Surely "to look on the sun by day" does not
mean "to look directly at the idea of the sun in the mind
by day." It means to look directly at the actually existing sun out there in the heavens. How could Locke know
where to direct his gaze unless he could perceive the sun
directly? But if direct perception of the sun is the obvious meaning of his words, then the problem of demonstrating the actual existence of the sun "through the intervention of his vivid idea" vanishes. Consequently
Locke again contradicts himself. Consistently with his
avowed principle that he "perceives nothing (directly)
but his own ideas" he could not "look on the sun by day."
For the sun is not the mere idea of the sun. To assert,
then, as Locke does, that he could perceive only the idea
of the sun and at the same time maintain that he perceives the actual sun is a contradiction.

For these reasons Locke fails to demonstrate the existence of bodies. This conclusion is confirmed by the
judgment of two philosophers of his own English school.

Professor Archibald Alexander sums up his study of
Locke thus:—"The truth is that Locke failed to make the
transition from the individual to the world, or from the
world to the individual. * * * All our knowledge is really
subjective according to Locke, and human certainty is
only relative certainty." (Hist. of Phil., pp. 216-217.)

Professor Green in his "Introduction to Hume's Treatise on Human Nature," section 59, gives the following
estimate of Locke's arguments to prove the existence of
objects outside of him. He says:—"Only if existence

were itself an idea would the consciousness of the agreement of the idea with it be a case of knowledge; but to make existence an idea is to make the whole question about the agreement of ideas, as such, with existence as such, unmeaning. * * * There can be no assurance of agreement between an idea and that which is no object of consciousness at all. * * * The raising of the question, in fact, as Locke puts it, implies the impossibility of answering it. It cannot be raised with any significance, unless existence is external to, and other than, an idea."

If, then, knowledge is, as Locke explicitly defines it, the perception of the agreement or disagreement of ideas, it logically follows that, when Locke declares "I exist," or "objects outside of me exist," both the subjects "I" and "objects outside of me," and the predicate "exist" are only *ideas*. (Hence it follows that both his own existence, and the existence of bodies outside of him are only *idea-existences*, and not actual existences.)

Locke wavered in attributing to "the notice we have of things by the senses" the name of "knowledge." For knowledge in Locke's terminology signified "absolutely certain knowledge," of which he seems to say that sense-knowledge of external bodies falls short. He says:—"The notice we have by our senses of the existence of things without us, though it be not altogether so certain as our intuitive knowledge, or the deductions of our reason employed about the clear abstract ideas of our own minds, yet it is an *assurance* that deserves the name of *knowledge*." (B IV—XI, 3.) On this passage Krauth comments:—"Now as the first of these (intuition) is not more than knowledge, the second and third must be less than knowledge, because they are less than the first. Locke feels this, and hence the rhetorical vagueness 'it is an assurance that *deserves the name* of knowledge' — it is really faith, not knowledge." (Berkeley, "Principles of Knowledge," p. 23.) It is, therefore, difficult to understand how Locke could prove the existence of God or of other people.

Locke was a typical Englishman. He gloried in inconsistencies. He muddled through his "Essay" somehow. He was also a true Puritan insofar as he was actually one thing — a Subjectivist, and professed to be another thing — a Realist. We are not surprised, then, that the strain of Subjectivism, inaugurated by Locke, and based upon two unproved assumptions, (1) the direct objects of knowledge are ideas, and (2) the mind cannot transcend itself so as to know something beyond its own states, has persisted in English thought from the days of Locke to our own time.

John Stuart Mill reduced all existence to *"Subjective"* sensation, and the "permanent possibility of sensation."

Huxley says, "It admits to no doubt that all our knowledge is a knowledge of States of Consciousness!"

"Again, the prevailing doctrine," says Bain, "is that a tree is something in itself apart from all perception. Yet what it may be anterior to, or independent of all perception, we cannot tell."

And Bradley, in his work "Appearance and Reality" teaches "there is no being or fact outside that which is commonly called psychical existence."

The Epistemological basis of Pragmatism teaches a like doctrine, that nothing exists but "streams of consciousness" murmuring onward in a bed of nothingness. Even moral obliquity, in their theory, is only a state of consciousness and nothing more, the innocent consequence of weakness, as Sir Oliver Lodge, the prophet of Ether, is now soothingly saying to remorse-bitten spirits, who have not yet crossed the great divide. Royce, the late professor of Harvard says, "The world is such stuff as ideas are made of."

In our day, J. S. Haldane, Fellow of Oxford, in his recent book "Mechanism, Life and Personality," says:— "The world we know is the world that appears to us in consciousness." Again, "The claim sometimes made in behalf of natural science, that its interpretations represent actual reality, cannot be maintained."

Another accomplished writer of the day, and undoubtedly an able physicist, Sir Oliver Lodge, tells us that "philosophers teach us that whatever we are primarily and directly aware of is not anything external, but a state of our own mind or consciousness. External reality is an inference or deduction from that. And though all our experience is based on reality, the reality may be very unlike our conception of it."[1] This, of course, is the sophism of Descartes and the false principle that has poisoned all modern thought.

[1]Cf. "The Triumph of Life", Barry, p. 17.

CHAPTER III

SENSISM OF LOCKE

Locke's Philosophical System (Continued)

IN the last chapter we have seen that the logical and inevitable consequence of Locke's gratuitous adoption of Descartes' idealistic postulate—gratuitous because it was accepted dogmatically by Locke without the slightest criticism or examination—was Idealism. (cf. Case—Physical Realism, p. 15.) That Locke clearly and explicitly adopted this postulate or supposition in answer to the question—"What do we know"? is manifest in the following statements. Locke says, "Idea serves best for *whatsoever is the object* of the understanding when a man thinks" (Introd. 8.) The objects of every man's thoughts, therefore, are only the ideas in the mind, not realities external to the mind. Again Locke asserts that "the mind hath no other immediate object but its own ideas, which it alone does or can contemplate." (IV. I. 1.) He repeats the same principle when he declares that, "all our knowledge consists in the view the mind has of its own ideas, which is the *utmost light and greatest certainty* we with our faculties and in our way of knowledge are capable of." (IV. II. 1.)

Yet Locke professed to be a Realist. Because he endeavored, as was explained in the last chapter, to make the transition by means of a reasoning process from his ideas in the mind to realities outside the mind. For he says—"The mind knows not things immediately but only by the intervention of the ideas it has of them." (IV. IV. 3.) This means that we *infer* the existence of the external world from the direct knowledge we have of our own subjective ideas. Locke was shrewd enough to see that this inferential process was beset with serious difficulty. For he says—"For having an idea of anything in our minds no more proves the existence of the thing than a picture of a man evidences his being in the world, or the vision of a dream makes thereby true history" (IV. VI. 11.) Premises constructed from the material of mere ideas can never yield a conclusion expressive of actual existence. How does Locke solve this difficulty? By frankly admitting that we have no real certainty of the existence of external objects. For he says—"General certainty is never to be found but in our ideas; it is the contemplation of our own abstract ideas that is alone able to afford us general knowledge," (IV. VI. 11), and then goes on to say that "The notice we have by our senses of the existence of things without us *is not altogether so certain* as our intuitive knowledge (i.e., the knowledge of axiomatic principles of the ideal order) or of the deductions of reason employed about the clear abstract ideas of our own minds, yet it is an *assurance* that deserves the name of knowledge." "The notice we have, then, by our senses of the existence of things without us" he calls not "Certainty" but Assurance," and thereby implies that "Assurance" falls short of the perfection of "Certainty." And since "Assurance" is not "Certainty," neither is it *Knowledge* proper, for in Locke's terminology, Knowledge and Certainty are synonymous. If this "Assurance," then, which we have of objects external to us through the senses is not knowledge and consequently not certain, what does this vague term "Assurance" mean? Locke says "it deserves the name of Knowledge." But it cannot. Krauth ("Berkeley's Principles of Knowledge," p. 23) interprets this "Assurance" not to be knowledge in the strict sense, but only *faith*. Hence Locke ultimately is driven to admit that the existence of the external world is not an object of *Knowledge* but an assumption of *blind faith*. "Blind faith" is a poor guarantee for the existence of the material world. In fact it is an insinuation on the part of Locke that it may not exist at all. This insinuation Berkeley and Hume afterwards developed into the absolute denial of the existence of the external world, and pushed Locke's principles to Idealism and Idealistic Phenomenalism. Berkeley, from a close study of Locke, showed that the latter had knowledge and certainty only of his own ideas, and that ideas were the materials of all his reasoning and knowledge. Hemmed in within the walled fortress of his own mind, Locke would be forever precluded from knowing anything of the outside world, which is distinct from, and something other than his own ideas, and absolute subjectivism could not be avoided. Logically, but falsely, Locke was an idealist, illogically, but sanely and rightly, he professed to be a realist. Locke began with the false principle that he knew nothing but his own ideas, and ends by declaring truly, that he knows also actually existing things beyond and distinct from, his own ideas. So impervious to a sense of logic and consistency is the muddling mentality of this "typical Englishman,"[1] that when logical it goes wrong, and when illogical it goes right. Other minds which are instinctively consistent wonder why Locke, when he discovered the *fact* that his objects of knowledge were more extensive than mere ideas, did not modify his hypothetical assumption that "he knew *nothing* but his own ideas," so as to harmonize with the fact that he professed to *know more* than his ideas, or else consistently maintain his hypothetical principle and honestly declare himself an idealist. The truth is that Locke repudiated principle. Yet reasonable men fully approve of the old Confucian proverb:— "better be poisoned in one's blood, than to be poisoned in one's principles.

Since Locke in his investigation of human knowledge began, in imitation of Descartes, with ideas, the main purpose of his "Essay" was an "inquiry into their original (origin)."

"Let us suppose," he says, "the mind to be, as we say, white paper, void of all character, without any ideas:— How comes it to be furnished? Whence comes it by that vast store which the busy and boundless fancy of man has painted on it with almost endless variety? Whence has it all the *materials* of reason and knowledge? To this I

---

[1] Leslie Stephen, History of English Thought, p. 35.

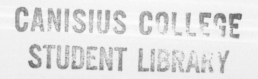

answer in one word, from *experience*. In that all our knowledge is founded; and from that it ultimately derives itself." (B II. I. 2.)

Locke, then, explains what he means by this ambiguous term "experience." "Our observation employed either about external sensible objects" (this channel of *experience* he calls "sensation" and the ideas conveyed through it he calls "the ideas of sensation") "or about the internal operations of our own minds perceived and reflected on by ourselves" (this second channel of *experience* he calls "reflection," and the ideas derived through it, he calls "ideas of reflection,") "is that which supplies our understandings with all the *materials* of thinking. These two (sensation and reflection) are the fountains of all knowledge, from whence all the ideas we have, or can naturally have, do spring." (Ibid.) Locke, then, will deny that the human mind possesses any ideas, except those that are directly brought into it by "sensation" and "reflection." For he says:—"These two, I say, viz., external things as the objects of *sensation,* and the operations of our own minds within, as the objects of REFLECTION are to me the only originals from whence all our ideas take their beginnings." (B II. C. I. 4.)

Remark the loose inconsistency of Locke expressed in the above passages. Previously he explicitly declared (Cf. Ch. II) that "ideas are the only direct objects of knowledge." Here he asserts, that "our observation is employed either about external objects, or about the internal operations of our own minds." But "external objects" are not "ideas," nor are the "internal operations," which are the objects of internal "reflection" identical with the "ideas," which these internal operations "imprint" on the understanding. Locke's theory of the origin of ideas is, that, just as external objects produce in the understanding "ideas of sensation," so "internal operations" produce also in the understanding "ideas of reflection." And in its reception of both classes of ideas the understanding, according to Locke, is entirely *passive*. For he says:—"The first capacity of the human intellect is, that the mind is fitted to receive in *the impressions made on it*, either through the senses by outward objects, or by its own operations when it reflects on them." (B II. C. I. 24.) And in paragraph 25 of the same chapter, he likens the understanding to a "mirror" which reveals its complete passivity, thus precluding the possibility of conceiving it as an active spiritual faculty. Notice also, that when he asserts that our observation is employed about "external objects," he is boldly and inconsistently begging the question. How does he, or can he know external objects by "observation employed about them," which supposes direct awareness of these objects, when he previously maintained that external objects are known by *inference* "through the intervention of ideas." How could he even perceive or know his own "internal operations," since these operations are not "ideas," but the causes or agencies that imprint in the understanding the "ideas of reflection." Yet Locke says in a passage quoted above that the "internal operations are the objects of reflection."

Yet, despite his inconsistencies, there stands out prominently in his system the great law which Locke endeavored to write into the constitution of his epistemology, which is to govern the origin of all human knowledge and to explain what he meant by "experience," namely, that all our knowledge is limited to these two aspects of "experience"—(1) sensation, (2) reflection. "All those sublime thoughts," he says, "which tower above the clouds, and reach as high as heaven itself, take their rise and footing here; in all that great extent wherein the mind wanders, in those remote speculations it may seem to be elevated with, it stirs not one jot beyond those ideas which *sense* (sensation) or *reflection* have offered for its contemplation." (B II. C. I. 24.)

What, then, according to Locke, is the nature or character of all the ideas which are derived from "experience" through the two channels of "sensation" and "reflection"? The answer to this question, based upon Locke's teaching, will decide whether his system, as it is traditionally regarded, is "exaggerated Sensism" in opposition to the "exaggerated intellectualism" of the Cartesians, and to the "moderate intellectualism" or "empirico-intellectualism" of the Scholastics—the three outstanding systems of history.

We shall now set forth the proofs to show that all the simple ideas that are derived through "sensation" and "reflection" are sensuous. And since these simple or unanalyzable ideas of "sensation" and "reflection" furnish all the materials of (man's) various knowledge it will follow that all our knowledge is sensuous. "I desire any one to assign any simple idea" he says, "which is not received from one of these inlets ("sensation" and "reflection") before mentioned, or any complex idea not *made out of those simple ones.* Nor will it be strange to think these few simple ideas sufficient to furnish the materials of all that various knowledge if we consider how many words may be made out of the various composition of twenty-four letters." (B. II. C. III. 10.) If then, the "ideas of sensation," and the "ideas of reflection" are both sensuous, it logically follows that all human knowledge, which, according to Locke is only a combination of simple sensuous ideas, just as words are a combination of the letters of the alphabet, is also sensuous.

Now, no one can question that all the ideas of sensation are sensuous. The very terms—"ideas of sensation" manifest the sensuous nature of those ideas. Locke explicitly calls the ideas derived from sensation a "sensation." "Thus," he says, "the perception which actually accompanies and is annexed to any impression on the body made by an external object furnishes the mind with a distinct idea which we call "sensation;" which is, as it were the actual entrance of any idea into the understanding by the senses." (B. II. C. XIX-1.) Locke in this passage explicitly calls the "idea" in question "a sensation." This seems conclusive in deciding that he considers the "ideas of sensation," which find "an entrance into the understanding by the senses," sensuous. And since "the perception which actually accompanies any impression on

the body furnishes the mind (i.e. the understanding) with
an idea, which we call "sensation," hence the mind or
understanding as the passive recipient of "sensation" is
really a sensuous faculty."

There is between the "active intellect" of Scholasticism
which, by the light it throws upon the sensuous phantasm
and by the process of abstraction, elevates the "species"
which it impresses upon the "possible intellect" to the
sphere of the supersensible, and the utter passivity of
Locke's "understanding" in its reception of ideas a striking contrast. For Locke says—"In this part (i.e. the part
that it plays in the reception of simple ideas) the understanding is merely passive" (B. II. C. I. 25.) Since then
in the reception of any idea of sense into the understanding, the latter is merely passive, this idea of sense being
sensuous remains sensuous when received into the passive
understanding since Locke recognizes no active function
in the intellect to raise this idea of sense to the supersensible order.

All the knowledge, then, which Locke professes to acquire of bodies assumed to exist outside of him, is strictly
limited to sensuous knowledge obtained "through the intervention" of his "representative" "ideas of sensation."
This conclusion Locke himself confirms when he says—
"Yet I think it not possible for any one to imagine any
other qualities in bodies howsoever constituted, whereby
they can be taken notice of, besides sounds, tastes, smells,
visible and tangible qualities" (B. II. C. II. 3.) That is,
we can come "to take notice of," those aspects of bodies
only which can be heard, tasted, smelled, seen, touched.
Nay even he says we cannot "imagine" any other bodily
attributes. This quotation is decisive in determining that
Locke's "ideas of sensation" are thoroughly sensuous.
Nay more, it implies that we possess no cognitive faculty
such as the spiritual intellect to put us in touch with other
aspects of bodies which are impervious to the direct ken
of sense. Obsessed as he is by this brute sensism, we can
now readily understand why Locke was logically justified
in proclaiming that he could not know bodily substances,

bodily essences, or bodies functioning as causes. Because substance, essence or cause cannot as such, make any direct impression or motion upon the senses. They cannot produce "sensations" or "sensuous ideas." Substance, essence, cause, because they are neither "proper" or "common" objects of any sense, cannot be known directly by any sense. They can be known, in virtue of themselves (per se) by intellect alone in its Aristotelian and Scholastic sense, exercising the double functions of the "active" and "possible" intellect. Hence Locke's meaning of intellect or understanding and the meaning attached to it by Scholasticism are entirely different. In Scholasticism intellect, in one phase of its functions, is intensely active. In Locke's system intellect or understanding is, in every phase of its functions decidedly passive. What Locke calls understanding is capable of receiving into it only sensuous or sensible ideas, the understanding or intellect of Scholasticism, because of the intense activity of the "active" intellect, is capable of grasping the sensible in a supersensible way. A former quotation (B. II. C. I. 5) is sufficient to show that Locke regarded the intellect or understanding as entirely passive. The following quotation emphasizes this passivity. Locke says:—"These simple ideas (i.e. of "sensation" and "reflection") when offered to the mind, the understanding can no more refuse to have, *nor alter when they are imprinted* than a *mirror* can refuse, *alter*, or obliterate the images or ideas, which the objects set before it do there produce" (B. II. C. I. 25.) Notice the suggestion of passivity in the terms "imprinted" and "mirror." Remark also that "ideas" in the understanding are like "images" in a mirror. When, therefore, outside bodies, which Locke assumes, make impressions or motions in some part of the body, and these impressions or motions, in turn, imprint passively their effects in the "mirror" of the understanding, effects which Locke calls "ideas of sensation," these ideas must be of the same nature as the cause that impresses them, just as the "images or ideas" reflected in a mirror are of the same nature "as the objects set before it do there produce."

Therefore are the "ideas of sensation" all sensuous, because they are the imprinted effects passively received in the understanding of motions or impressions on the body, which are certainly sensuous.

Now, before examining the further problem,—whether Locke's "ideas or reflection" are also sensuous, it will be instructive to indicate some manifestly false interpretations of sense—knowledge, which are frequently met with in our author's "Essay."

Locke assumes, in the first place, that his "ideas of sensation" represent only the sensuous singular qualities of external objects. He then attempted to demonstrate though unsuccessfully, "through the intervention of (these) ideas," the actual existence of sensuous singular qualities outside the mind. And since Locke taught that substance was a mere creation or figment of the mind—"the idea, then," he says we have to which we give the general name substance being nothing but the *supposed,* but *unknown* support of these qualities which we find existing, which we *imagine* cannot subsist *sine re substante*—without something to support them—we call that support *substantia* (B II. C. XXIII. 2), he consequently looked upon bodies as a mere *cluster* or *bundle of singular qualities*, and that these qualities were the only objects of sense—knowledge. "And thus we come (i.e. through sensation) by those ideas we have of yellow, white, heat, cold, soft, hard, bitter, sweet and all those which we call sensible qualities." (B II. C. I. 3.) Was each of these qualities which Locke conceived as constituting existing bodies, abstractions or abstracts? They certainly were. Locke, of course, did not mean that each quality in an actual body was the object of an abstract, universal idea, because Locke as a sensist did not admit genuinely universal ideas, (B. IV. C. XVII. 8) much less that such ideas had "a foundation in reality." Each quality was, indeed, for Locke a singular, determinate quality. But each of those singular qualities were still abstractions or abstracts.

Because an abstract means "a quality without a subject." And surely each of Locke's singular qualities was really a quality without a *subject* or *qualified,* or a *substance.* Hence each quality of the cluster existing together in a body was an *abstract,* a singular abstract indeed, but still an abstract.

Of course, Locke was mistaken when he taught that the senses perceive only the singular qualities of bodies, isolated or abstracted from the bodily substance. A little reflection will convince any realist that what the senses perceive in the natural order, is never a quality, even a singular quality, but the whole concrete body or qualified under the formality of some primary (common object of sense) or secondary (proper object of sense) quality. For instance nobody ever perceived by the sense of sight this color apart or abstracted from the colored object. "Non percipimus colorem," says Sanseverino sed color-atum."[1] In an object of sense-perception the formal objects of the senses are not isolated or abstracted from the material objects of the senses. Both are perceived in the concrete, that is lumped together. Hence Sanseverino says:—"Atque in primis, nos per sensus qualitates non in universum consideratum, sed determinatum, hoc est aliquid coloratum. Jamvero qualitates nonnisi per sub-jectum sunt concretae et determinatae. Ergo si quali-tates et concretas et determinatas percepimus, nos non solum qualitates sensiles (as Locke maintained,) sed *etiam substantiam* in qua ipsae inhaerent, sentire pro certo habendum est."[2] Hence the senses perceive not only the sensible qualities of bodies but also the substance in which they are concreted.

The senses of course do not perceive the substance *as such,* because the substance as such is not the formal object of any sense. Substance as such is an object *per se* of intellect alone. Yet the senses perceive what is *in fact* a substance accidentally (*per accidens*) as their "ma-terial," though not as their "formal object." In an object

[1-2]Cf. Sanseverino, Dynamologia, Vol. I, pp. 362-3; Geny, Critica, p. 174; Maritain, Introd. to Phil., p. 226.

of sense perception the "material object" is never isolated
from the "formal objects" of sense perception. That the
senses perceive the substance *indirectly* (per accidens)
through its qualities never crossed Locke's vision, though
it is the common teaching of Scholasticism. ✓

We now approach the problem of Locke's "ideas of reflection." Are the "ideas of reflection" in Locke's system
also sensuous?

Locke, in the following passages, explains his "ideas
of reflection." He writes:—"Secondly, the other fountain
from which experience furnisheth the understanding with
ideas is—the perception of the operations of our own
minds within us, as it is employed *about the ideas it has
got*; which operations, when the soul comes to reflect on
and consider, do furnish the understanding with another
set of ideas, which could not be had from things without.
And such are perception, thinking, doubting, believing,
reasoning, knowing, willing, and all the different actings
of our minds, which we being conscious of, and observing
in ourselves, do from these (operations) receive into our
understandings as distinct ideas as we did from bodies
affecting our sense." (B. II. C. I. 4.) This new set of
ideas Locke calls the "ideas of reflection," and he understands by "reflection" "the perception of internal operations."

Again Locke says:—"In time the mind comes to reflect on its own operations *about the ideas got by sensation,* and thereby stores itself with a new set of ideas,
which I call ideas of reflection." (Ibid. 24.)

Just, then, as the understanding receives passively,
according to Locke, one set of ideas, namely the "ideas of
sensation" arising "from our observation employed about
external objects" whose existence Locke assumes though
he never directly perceives them, for what he professes
to perceive immediately are his ideas, so do we receive
passively into the same understanding another set of ideas
which he calls "ideas of reflection," arising from "our perception of the operations within us" "about the ideas already got by sensation."

The considerations and arguments that go to show that these "ideas of reflection" are, like the "ideas of sensation" wholly sensuous, are cumulative in their persuasiveness.

In the first place, Locke describes "reflection" as "the perception of the operations of our own minds within us as it (perception) is employed about the ideas got by sensation." (B. II. C. I. 4.) What then is the specific nature of those "operations" that are the direct and immediate objects of "perception" in the act of "reflection." The nature of an act or "operation" is determined and specified by the kind or nature of the objects about which this act or "operation" is directly and immediately employed, that is, by the *formal object* of such an act or "operation." What then, is the nature of the direct and immediate objects of the operations which are perceived in an act of reflection?" Locke answers by saying that the "operations" that is, the direct and immediate objects of "perception" in the act of "reflection" are *about the ideas got by sensation.*" Now these ideas of sensation, are, as we have already shown, entirely sensuous. Therefore, are the "operations" employed about these "ideas of sensation" likewise sensuous. But if the "operations" are sensuous, so must the "perception" of them be also sensuous, since they are the direct and immediate objects—the formal objects—of that "perception." The "perception," then, "of the operations of our own minds within us," that is, "reflection," demands no higher faculty than sense. Hence we conclude that both the "ideas of reflection," as well as the "ideas of sensation," are sensuous. This conclusion is confirmed by the teaching of Locke, that the understanding is "entirely passive," (B. II. C. I. 24,) and that all representative ideas" are *particular,* as well as by the peculiar Lockean doctrines described in the following paragraphs.

Locke, in discussing one of the most important operations of the human mind, namely *reasoning,* which is the prerogative of man, says:—"Every man's reasoning and knowledge is (sic) only about the ideas existing in his

own mind, which are truly, *every one of them particular
existences*. And our knowledge and reasoning about other
things is only as they correspond with these *our particular
ideas*. So that the perception of the agreement or disagreement of our *particular ideas* is the whole and utmost
of all our knowledge. Universality is but accidental to it,
and consists only in this, that the particular ideas about
which it is, are such as more than one particular thing
can correspond with and be represented by." (B. IV.
C. XVII. 8.)

Locke, in this passage, clearly states that all our ideas
represent "particular existences," that is, individually existing sensuous "qualities." "The perception of the agreement or disagreement of our particular ideas is the whole
and utmost of all our knowledge." The fact that Locke
teaches that *all our ideas* are particular, that is, singular,
and that universality is not essential to any one of them,
is a presumptive indication that we possess no spiritual
faculty of intellect, which alone could form universal
ideas, and that sense faculties alone are sufficient to account for particular or singular, that is, sensuous ideas.
But since, as Locke maintains, that "all our knowledge"
supposes only particular or singular ideas, that is sensuous ideas, then the "ideas of reflection" which make up
one class of Locke's ideas, must also be sensuous.

Even Fraser, the editor of the best edition of Locke's
"Essay," and who is no apologist for Scholasticism, com-
menting on the passage just quoted, says in a note:—
"Locke fails to distinguish between ideas as sense-phenomena, and ideas as concepts and meanings. And how
can any inference (of reasoning) be made if particulars
per se are our sole original data"? If Locke then recognizes that we can know only *sense-phenomena*, all his
ideas, both those of "sensation" and "reflection," are
sense-ideas or sensuous.

In another passage Locke says:—"This source of ideas
(reflection) every man has within himself, and though it
be not a sense, as having nothing to do with external objects (i.e. not an external sense); yet it (reflection) is

very like it and *might properly enough* be called "*internal sense.*" (B. II. C. I. 4.)

It is true that the term "sense" is in the English language, sometimes interpreted not as a sense faculty, but is used metaphorically to signify what is really an intellectual faculty, as in the expressions "common sense" and "moral sense." But no one would say, except a Sensist, that the word "sense" in these expressions might properly enough be called a "sense." On the contrary when Locke calls "reflection" properly enough an internal sense," he suggests, especially if we keep in mind his other quotations, that it is really a sense in its own right and nature.

The consequences of this "Exaggerated Sensism" of Locke are fatal to science. For science is of the universal, and Sensism destroys all knowledge of the universal. Sensism cannot transcend the experience of the past and present; science professes to know what will happen in the future. No man can sensuously experience the future. Yet when men assert even the simple law that "fire burns," they express a universal physical truth. They mean and know that by its nature, "fire will burn" to-morrow, as it does today.

Sensism destroys all religion. The existence of God is the fundamental truth of religion. Hence Locke's Sensism logically leads, as it did in fact lead in the subsequent philosophy of Herbert Spencer in the nineteenth century in England, to Agnosticism. And Agnosticism in turn is destructive of morality. No wonder we witness today a growing deterioration of morals. Locke's Sensism, as we shall see, subsequently developed into Positivism (Compte), Phenomenalism and Scepticism (Hume), Idealism (Berkeley), and Materialism (French Encyclopedists).

CHAPTER IV

LOCKE'S IDEA OF SUBSTANCE

Locke's Philosophical System (Continued)

IN the last chapter we have seen that Locke professed to derive all his ideas both "simple" and "complex" from "*experience*," through the double fountain of "sensation" and "reflection." Both his "ideas of sensation," and his "ideas of reflection" were, in their nature, proved to be sensuous. Locke, therefore, interpreted experience as presenting to the mind only those aspects of reality which, by virtue of themselves (per se,) affect directly and stimulate the sense-faculties, completely ignoring other aspects of reality contained in the data of experience which transcend the senses, but which intellect or reason, which is the same faculty, is capable of discovering. Consequently Locke would strictly limit all that the human mind can know within the narrow field of sense-knowledge. This, of course, is brute sensism.

But Locke was a conservative. He frankly acknowledged that his mind was furnished by a whole department of ideas which were the traditional heritage of the human race, and embedded in the grammar and expressed in the languages of all civilized peoples. Yet these ideas represent neither "proper" nor "common" objects of any sense whether external or internal, and could not, therefore, be accounted for as "ideas or sensation" or "ideas of reflection." Such are the ideas of "substance," "cause," "universality," "necessity," "infinity," "omnipotence," "eternity," spirit or soul, God, etc. These ideas are not *impressed* upon the understanding either by outward objects or by internal operations. Locke, passionately wedded to Sensism, was at his wit's ends to account for the origin of those ideas. They are all of their very nature *supersensible*. They transcend sense. Hence, were men endowed with sense-faculties only,—a doctrine which Locke endeavored to popularize,—then his mind could never be furnished with the ideas which we have enumerated. These ideas could not be innate, for Locke repudiated innate ideas.

Yet Locke admits he posseses those ideas. How, then, does he account for their origin? Locke's answer to this question will be enlightening, because it will reveal the peculiar characteristics of the main trend at least of the philosophy of the English school, of which Locke was a typical exponent.

Now, in reviewing the history of human thought we discover that there are three classical and outstanding theories to explain the origin of those supersensible ideas which we have previously indicated.

(1) The first theory is, that such ideas as substance, cause, etc. were not derived in any conceivable manner whatsoever from sense-experience. Recall Plato's theory of ideas; Descartes' innate ideas, or at least innate in the sense that they were the offsprings of the mind on the *occasion* of sense-experience; Malebranche's intuitional perception of them in God's essence, and the thorough-going innateness of all ideas in the theory of Leibnitz. Even Kant's explanation of their origin, as we shall see later, was really only a modified form of Descartes' innate ideas.

(2) In opposition to the extreme view that all ideas that transcend sense-experience are innate or congenital to the mind, is the equally extreme theory that all ideas are on the same level with, and derived from "experience," meaning by experience nothing more than *sense-experience*. That is, the *data* or what is given in experience is always either a "proper" or "common object" of some sense-faculty, objects, therefore, *per se* of sense. According to this theory, all ideas objectively considered are *formally* contained in sense-experience, and hence ideas subjectively considered are referred to some sense-faculty. In other words there are no other modes or aspects of reality in experience capable of being known by the human mind, except what the senses can discover. Hence all our ideas whether they come into the mind through the chan-

nel of "sensation" or "reflection" are, every one of them, sensuous, individual or particular.   This is true, in this theory, whether we consider the "simple ideas" that the senses first grasp, or their combinations or compounds afterwards formed by the union of "simple ideas." For any combination of "simple, sensuous ideas" can form only more complex ideas which are of the same nature or kind, namely sensuous as the elements from which they were formed. This is Locke's theory of *Sensism*. In Locke's explanation, then, there is no place for those intellectual or supersensible concepts that transcend sense.   All ideas are sensuous, and there are no ideas or concepts which are not sensuous.   This doctrine Locke professes explicitly to teach in his famous challenge wherein he says:—"Let any one examine his own thoughts, and thoroughly search into his understanding; and then let him tell me, whether all the original ideas he has there, are any other than of the objects of his senses, or of the operations of his mind, considered as objects of reflection. And how great a mass of knowledge soever he imagines to be lodged there, he will, upon taking a strict view, see that he has not any idea in his mind but what one of these two have (sic) imprinted: —though perhaps, with infinite variety compounded and enlarged by the understanding." (B. II. C. I-5.)   Frazer, the editor of the best edition of Locke's Essay, in a note on this passage, asks the significant question—"Does this limitation of our ultimate sources of experience make the *"Essay"* an expression of the materialistic formula 'Every man counts as an animal, and *no man can count for more than an animal* ?"

(3) The third classical theory to explain the origin of ideas is a "via media" between the theory of Innatism and Locke's Sensism. This explanation of the origin of ideas is attributed to Aristotle and adopted by Scholasticism. It maintains, in general, with Locke, that all ideas and all knowledge have their ultimate source and *beginning* in *sense-experience.   "Nihil est in intellectu nisi prius fuerit aliquo modo in sensu."* By "sense-experience" Locke understands the *mediate* cognition of a cluster of *primary,*

singular per se qualities in a body but without a *qualified,* whereas the common teaching of Scholasticism is that "sense experience" is the immediate cognition of a singular object in the *concrete.* Both Locke and the Scholastics, therefore, agree on the same point of departure to explain the source or fountain of all the ideas which the human mind is naturally capable of acquiring. But while Locke and the Sensists would say, that all the ideas objectively considered, which the human mind is capable of knowing are contained *formally* in sense-experience, and, therefore, that all natural knowledge is sense-knowledge only, the scholastics on the other hand would say, that all the ideas, objectively considered, which the human mind is naturally capable of acquiring, are contained either *formally,* or somehow *materially* in sense-experience, that is, in the objective something perceived concretely by sense.

Locke and the Sensists recognize that human beings possess only sense-faculties wherewith all ideas that can be acquired, are acquired. The scholastics, on the other hand, recognize that human beings possess a cognitive faculty superior to sense, viz:—intellect, or reason which is the same faculty, and that this superior faculty is capable of recognizing in the objects of sense-experience *other aspects of reality* which are impervious to the ken of sense. In other words, the objects of sense are so many outward signs or natural sacramentals veiling inner, permanent, essential aspects of reality which, to the senses are, by virtue of themselves (per se), wholly hidden, but which to intellect are (per se) revealed and from the first and immediate ideas of certain aspects of reality revealed by intellect in the *material* object of sense, such as substance, cause, etc., the same intellect by negation and analogy can acquire the loftiest ideas of spirit, God, etc. Let us now return to the task of setting forth and critically examining Locke's attempt to account for the origin, in harmony with his Sensism, of one of the most fundamental ideas of which every human mind acknowledges the possession—the idea of substance. The real existence of substance is vital to all sound philosophy but especially to Catholics. On its real existence depends the truth of the Blessed Sacrament.

Locke never got rid of the idea, at least, of substance, as Berkeley partially, and Hume completely did. It obsessed him and he could never exorcise it from his mind.

Consistently with the courageous challenge quoted above, Locke professed to derive all his ideas from the senses, either through "external sensation" (ideas of sensation), or through "reflection" upon our internal operations exercised, as he says, upon the ideas already "got through sensation" (ideas of reflection), or through both. Could Locke succeed in deriving the idea of substance from either "sensation" or "reflection"? He could not. The reason is obvious. We have previously made manifest that Locke was a Sensist, that is, he professedly taught that all the ideas which he possessed, and which are truly representative of existing realities are derivable through sense-faculties only. "Ideas of sensation" came through the external senses, and "ideas of reflection" are derived from what he calls "properly enough an internal sense." Since Locke, then, recognized only sense-faculties of cognition, and since it is obvious that "substance" is not capable of *directly stimulating* or making any impression upon any sense-faculty, either as a "proper" or "common object" of sense, it follows that it is impossible for substance, which, in an object of sense, intellect or reason alone can in itself and through itself (per se) discover, to be an idea either of "sensation" or "reflection," in other words, to be a sensuous idea.

Locke himself explicitly admits this conclusion when he says:—"the idea of substance we neither have nor can have by "sensation" or "reflection" (I. IV.-18.) Besides the reason already given, there is, in Locke's theory of "Representative Realism" another obvious reason why we neither have nor can have the idea of substance by "sensation" or "reflection." "Sensation" according to Locke brings into the mind ideas which represent only *qualities* in external bodies, and "reflection" ideas which are copies of our internal "*operations*." But neither mere "qualities" of bodies, or "operations" of the soul, are substances. For neither can exist by virtue of themselves (per se) or in themselves (in se), a mode of existence which substance necessarily demands. We are speaking of created substance. And when the phrase "by virtue of itself" is applied to created substance, it does not mean of course, that it has no cause, but simply that it exists by itself or in itself and not in another.[1] A compelling necessity forces upon the mind the absolute impossibility in the natural order, for a quality like "motion" for example, to exist without a moving object, or a "thought" to exist without a thinker. How then, did this strange interloper, the idea of substance, find a place in his mind? Locke's explanation of the origin of this idea is in full accord with his brute Sensism and Occamite Nominalism. In B. II. C. XXIII. he divides the discussion of the origin of this idea into two parts. He first endeavors to explain how the mind arrives at the idea of a particular or individual substance, and secondly the origin of the general (universal) idea of substance—the first and second substances of Aristotle.

In explaining the ground on which he bases the origin of the idea of a particular or singular substance, he says:

"The mind being, as I have declared, furnished with a great number of the simple ideas conveyed in by the senses, as they are found in exterior things, or by reflection on its own operations, takes notice also, that a certain number of those simple ideas go constantly together; which being *presumed* to belong to one thing, and words being suited to common apprehensions, and made use of for quick dispatch, are called, so united in one subject, by one name, which by *inadvertency*, we are apt afterward to talk of and consider as one simple idea, which indeed is a complication of many ideas together; because as I have said, *not imagining how these simple ideas can subsist by themselves*, we *accustom* ourselves to *suppose* some *sub-*

---

[1] Maritain, Introd. to Phil., pp. 218-224.

stratum wherein they do subsist, and from which they do result, which therefore, we call 'substance'." (II. XXIII. 1.)

To understand some phrases in this curious explanation of how the idea of substances arises in the mind, we must bear in mind that Locke professed to belong to the school of "Representative Realism." We say "professed to belong," because were Locke logical and consistent, he should have been, like Hume, a "Phenomenal Idealist." The "Representative Realism" of Locke assumes with Descartes in the first place, that ideas within the mind, not objects outside the mind, are the direct and immediate objects of our knowledge, and secondly, that "ideas of sensation" image forth only certain *qualities* existing outside of us, and "ideas of reflection" mirror only *operations* within us. We never, according to Locke, perceive directly either the outside *qualities* themselves, nor the *operations* of the mind directly in themselves, but only the *images* or *representations* of both in our ideas. Locke then assumes that we know the really existing *qualities* of bodies and our own internal *operations* "through the intervention of the ideas" of them, because the ideas represent or mirror forth both the *qualities* and the *operations*.

In Locke's terminology, then, ideas as "representations" are of course in the mind, while what they profess to represent are really existing "qualities" outside of us, or really existing "operations" of the mind. He distinguishes between "subjective ideas" which are representations in the mind and "objective ideas" which are existing "qualities" or "operations" of which the ideas within the mind are copies. Yet he tantalizingly uses the one term "idea" without any indication of whether he wishes it to be understood in a subjective or objective sense. For instance, when he says in the above quotation—"the mind being furnished with a great number of simple ideas conveyed in by the senses," "simple ideas" are taken in a subjective sense. Whereas, in the next phrase—"as they (the ideas) are found in exterior things," it is obvious that he means "ideas" in an objective sense, as synonymous with really existing "qualities" or "operations" of the mind outside and independent of the subjective ideas of them.

Examining the above quotation and similar passages wherein he treats of the idea of substance, we shall find that Locke, as a thorough-going Sensist, recognizes that those ideas alone that come into the mind through the double channel of "sensation" and "reflection" represent all that we can know of any existing object. Hence Locke insists that we have no ideas, clear or otherwise, of what actually exists, except those that represent a cluster or bundle of "qualities" in bodies, and a collection of "operations" in themselves. Every other aspect of reality is *unknown* to us. Hence "substance" is *"unknown,"* because we can have no idea of it from either "sensation" or "reflection." What, then, can Locke mean by "mind" in the phrase—"The mind being furnished with a great number of simple ideas"? What can he mean by "exterior things" in the phrase—"As they (the ideas) are found in exterior things." Locke can mean nothing more by mind than a collection or series of "operations" without an "operator," "a stream of consciousness" apart from anyone being conscious. This theory of mind is, of course, "Idealistic Phenomenalism," the very theory to which Hume, as we shall see, reduced Locke's philosophy.

By "exterior things" Locke can mean only a cluster of sensuous "qualities," without a "qualified" or substance. This is the theory that is known as Positivism.

Yet Locke admits he posssesses the idea of substance, otherwise it could never have occurred to him to write so much about it. He is, then, at his wits' end to account for its origin and presence in his mind. So, what does he do? Without the slightest evidence or ground of reason, he regards "substance" as a *creation and invention of the understanding*, a purely mental phantom, that, as far as he knows, has no actual existence outside the mind at all. For, in the above quotation, he accounts for its origin by

an act of "supposition" or "inadvertency, (which) we
are apt afterward to talk of and consider as *one* simple
idea, which indeed is a *complication* of many ideas together." Since a "supposition" is nothing more than a
mental conjecture or fancy, and an invention of the imagination, Locke bases his idea of "substance" on a merely
phantom creation of the mind, that has no real existence.
Thus, for Locke, the idea of "substance" is in no way
determined by any existing object. Were Locke logically
consistent, he should have forthwith rejected "substance,"
as distinct from *qualities*, as an empty fiction, and acknowledged only as real a bundle or cluster of "qualities"
or "operations of the mind" existing by virtue of themselves (per se) and in themselves (in se), and thus fall
into the absurd extreme of making both "qualities" and
"operations" as they exist in the natural order "substances."

Again when Locke grounds his idea of "substance"
upon an "inadvertency" of mind "by which we talk of
and consider as one idea (substance), which is indeed a
complication of many ideas together," he conceals under
the vague terms "inadvertency," "talk of" and "consider"
what is truly for him a *deception*. But if "substance"
and the "idea of substance" is a product of "deception,"
then have we a corroborative proof that Locke considered
"substance" as a fictitious creation of his mind, and should
have rejected substance and openly claimed with the Posi-
tivists that the only objects that exist in the world around
us are *clusters of qualities* without any "substantial
qualified."

Throughout an entire chapter—B. II. C. XXIII, Locke
wearisomely reiterates his attack on the real existence of
"substance," so far as the human mind is concerned, by
always insisting that it is a merely "supposed," "imagined," "unknown" support of "accidents," that is, of
"qualities" or "operations of mind"—a mere mental creation.

Yet in this same chapter Locke, exasperatingly inconsistent, coolly maintains that "sensation convinces us that

there are solid, extended substances; and reflection that there are thinking ones" (B. II. C. XXIII. 29.) Here he throws his "supposed," "imagined," "unknown" support of "accidents" to the winds, and declares that "sensation" provides him with a knowledge of material substances, and "reflection" of thinking substances, which he calls a "conviction." Yet in B. I. IV.-18, he previously said that "the idea of substance" we neither have nor can have by "*sensation*" and "*reflection*." And since these are the only channels which Locke recognizes to bring all that we can know to the mind, it follows that if the knowledge of "substance" cannot be brought into the mind through "sensation" or "reflection," we cannot have any knowledge of a real substance at all, much less a "conviction" of its existence.

The non-existence of "substance" he again insinuates in the following passage—"It is manifest that everyone upon inquiry into his own thoughts will find, that he has no other idea of any substance, v.g., let it be gold, horse, iron, man, vitriol, bread, but what he has barely of those *sensible qualities* which he *supposes* to inhere, with a *supposition* of such a *substratum* as gives, as it were, a support to these qualities or simple ideas which he has observed to exist united together. (B. II. C. XXIII. 6.) "Thus the idea of the sun, what is it but an aggregate of those several simple ideas—bright, hot, roundish, having a constant, regular motion, at a certain distance from us, and perhaps some others?" (Ibid.)

Hence Locke recognizes no other reality in bodies except a collection or cluster of "qualities," and no other reality in soul except a series of "operations," plus a fancied "supposition" of a "support," which, in each case has no actual existence, as far as he knows, beyond a mere phantom existence as a product of his own imagination.

It is strange that Locke had recourse to "supposition," "imagination," "custom" to account for his merely *subjective* idea or notion of substance, notwithstanding the fact that he stumbled upon, in the following passage, the *true, rational ground* on which to base the real existence

of substance. He says:—"Hence when we talk or think
of any particular sort of corporeal substance, as horse, or
stone, etc., though the idea we have of either of them be
*but the complication or collection of those several simple
ideas of sensible qualities,* which we used to find united in
the thing called 'horse' or 'stone'; yet BECAUSE WE
CANNOT CONCEIVE (in a former passage he used the
term "imagine" which he here changes into 'conceive'
thereby suggesting the exercise of reason) HOW THEY
SHOULD SUBSIST ALONE, NOR ONE IN ANOTHER,
we *suppose* them existing in, and supported by, some common subject, which support we denote by the name
'substance'.

If Locke had only pondered a little and reflected upon
the meaning of the phrase, *"because we cannot conceive,
etc.,"* he would have clearly understood the true ground
of reason upon which common sense could validly and
logically base the real existence and knowledge of the substance of his 'horse' or 'stone,' without having recourse
to his vapid 'supposition,' etc. For out there in the
"horse" or "stone" he professed at least to admit the actual existence of real qualities in those objects. For when
Locke wrote *"yet because we cannot conceive, how they*
(the objective, existing qualities) *should subsist alone,
nor one in another,"* a light of valid reason based on objective evidence, flashed upon his mind, which should have
led him to realize, that qualities could not exist alone by
virtue of themselves (per se), or in themselves (in se)
without a *qualified,* that is, a concrete substance. Such
a process of reasoning is not a "supposition" or a creation
of the mind, but a valid inference that carries with it the
guarantee of its own evidence for the real existence of
the substance of "horse" or "stone." For any inference
or conclusion of reason that is connected with what already exists—and Locke admitted the "qualities" and
"operations," really existed—by a *link of necessity,* must
itself also express what really exists. Just as, when we
observe something happening or coming into being, we
necessarily conclude that it must have a cause.

Not to admit such clear and necessarily compelling reasons would be the destruction of all science. But Locke was an inveterate Sensist. He could not, therefore, admit that he had any idea in his mind that did not come in there directly through a channel of sense, or any object outside his mind that did not directly stimulate or impress a sense. If he had such an idea, or imagined such an object outside his mind, he accounted for both by making them *a mere mental creation*. He would deny, consequently, that he could have any idea that is acquired by the superior faculty of intellect, or the real existence of any object that only reason could lead him to recognize. Locke, with so many modern scientists, repudiates any inference of reason that cannot be verified by sense-knowledge or experiment. In other words he would not admit that any supersensible object could come within the purview of what is knowable to him as a real existence. If, as he admits, he has ideas of supersensible objects, such ideas he would account for by a "supposition," "imagination," "custom," creations of his mind, the objects of which are entirely unknown. Of course this is the denial of Metaphysics. How Locke could account for the existence of God and the existence of the soul, which he yet professed to admit, it is difficult to understand.

The fundamental reason why Locke and so many modern philosophers deny or doubt the reality of substance, or assume towards its reality an agnostic attitude is, because they are Sensists, whether their Sensism takes the form of Positivism or Phenomenalism. The Positivistic Locke never realized that

"There is more in things than meets the eye."
His eagerness to refute the "Exaggerated Intellectualism" of Descartes as well as the Cambridge Platonists of his day, both of whom taught that we have a direct, immediate intuitional insight into the nature or essence of substance through innate ideas may have had a strong influence in precipitating him into the opposite extreme of "Exaggerated Sensism." Locke was quite right in rejecting this extreme intellectual claim of the Innatists. We

have no direct intuition of the nature of individual essences. But it does not follow that because the "Exaggerated Intellectualism" of the Cartesians is false, that
the opposite extreme of Locke's "Exaggerated Sensism"
is true. There is the "Moderate Intellectualism" of Scholasticism which is the true *via media* between these
extremes.

Nor does it follow that because we have no immediate,
intuitional knowledge of the nature of substance, that we
have no means, as Locke imagines, of arriving at a knowledge of their nature or essence. How, then, may we
arrive at some knowledge of the nature or essence of
substance?

So completely in harmony with common sense and
reason is the means at our disposal of gaining some insight into the nature and essence of substances, that, just
as Locke hit upon the rational principle by which he could
have legitimately arrived at a valid knowledge of the existence of substance, when he said "because we cannot
conceive ('conceive' suggests intellectual knowledge) how
qualities should subsist alone," though he passed heed-
lessly over the rational force of that principle, so also
does Locke stumble upon the key-principle that reveals to
us some knowledge of the *nature* and *essence* of substances, when he says:—"So that of substance, we have
no idea of what it is, but a confused, obscure idea of
what it does." (Letter to the Bishop of Worcester.)
Locke here saw the light, but he seemed to have shut his
eyes against it. We have surely a clear idea of "what a
substance does." We can observe its actions. We have
no intuitional knowledge, for example, of the character
of others. Yet we can arrive at such knowledge. How?
By simply observing *what they do*. Their actions reveal
what they are—"A tree is known by its fruit." Hence
we can validly infer what a substance is from what
it does. Scholasticism expresses this principle thus—
"*operari sequitur esse.*" We quote Dr. Coffey on the practical working of this simple principle—"As are their (substances) properties,—their activities, energies, qualities,

and all their accidents—so is their nature. We know of
the latter just what we can *infer* from the former—
operari sequitur esse; we have no other key than this to
the knowledge of their specific natures. We have experience of them only through their properties, their be-
havior, their activities; analysis of this experience, *a
posteriori reasoning* from it, inductive generalization
based upon it; such are the channels we possess, the only
means at our disposal, for reaching a knowledge of their
natures." (Ontol. pp. 218-9.) Thus do we arrive at a clear
idea both of the *existence* and nature or essence of substance through sense and intellect or reason.

CHAPTER V

INTELLECTUAL IDEAS IN LOCKE'S SYSTEM

Locke's Philosophical System (Continued)

WE have seen in the last chapter the vast difference between the meaning which Locke puts into the term "experience" and the interpretation given to it by Scholasticism. Both Locke and the Scholastics repudiate "innate ideas," whether such ideas are taken in the sense that they are fully formed inborn or congenital endowments of the mind from the beginning, as Locke seems to have understood them, or are the offsprings of the mind alone on the *occasion* of sense-experience, as Descartes seems to have taught. Locke and Scholasticism are also in accord in teaching that all human knowledge begins with sense-experience, and that, therefore, before the advent of sense-experience the mind is a "tabula rasa" - a clean slate without any ideas, But in the further and more detailed interpretation of the content of sense-experience as the initial source of all human knowledge Locke and the Scholastics part company.

Even should we grant that Locke had validly established his inferential or "reasoned-realism" through "the intervention of ideas" which were the direct and immediate object of his knowledge, still he would be obliged to maintain in harmony with his Sensism, that the full round of all the cognitive faculties of human nature is capable of knowing nothing more in an object of sense-experience than what directly (per se) affects the senses. That is, through "ideas of sensation," he professed to know certain sensuous "qualities" ("primary qualities" and "powers") of external objects, but never the "qualified," and through "ideas of reflection" he professed to know "internal operations" but never the "operator," because in each case Locke has explicitly declared that "substance" is *unknown*. Logically, then, Locke should

have honestly declared that he knew only "sensuous phenomena" alone, the very doctrine which Hume afterwards
derived from Locke's principles.   A study of the following
passages in his "Essay" clearly reveals this Sensism of
Locke - B II. 1. 2. 3. 4-5; B II. 1. 24; B II. II. 3; B II.
III. 10; B IV. XVII. 8.

Scholasticism, on the other hand, maintains that there
are other modes or aspects of reality in an object of sense-
experience besides those modes and aspects that directly
(per se) affect the senses.   And those modes or aspects
of an object of sense-experience which do not and cannot
directly (per se) but only *per accidens* affect the senses,
can, and do, if we may use the expression, affect the spiritual faculty of intellect *per se,* and are *per se* perceptible
by the intellect alone.   In a word there is in an object of
"experience" two realms of reality, clearly and distinctly
marked off from each other.   One of these realms of reality can be known both by sense and intellect, by sense
directly and *per se,* sensuously, by intellect intellectually.
Of the other realm the senses can have no direct, *per se*
knowledge, but only an indirect *per accidens* knowledge,
whereas of the second realm the intellect enjoys a mon-
opoly of its own *per se* knowledge over all the realities
that are there discoverable by intellect alone.   Such realities in an object of sense-experience are *substance, cause,
necessity, universality,* etc.   The realities and aspects of
reality within the domain of intellect are just as objectively real, and far more important in life than the realities within the domain of sense.   I wish I were a humor-
ist.   For there is a rich field for humor in that persistent
attack on reason and intellect since the days of Luther,
which is so zealous to make us animals and only animals.
This tendency seems to be an expression of jealousy
against Catholics who have ever defended intellect and
will continue to do so, because they vindicate a power
within us which lifts us to a dignity little less than that
of the angels.

Locke has been a leader in this attack.   He confesses
he possesses intellectual ideas, such as those of substance,

cause, necessity, universality, spirit, God, etc. But the senses cannot formulate such ideas. Hence he will relegate the realities which intellectual ideas represent to the realm of fairy phantoms and superstitious myths. Sensism of course denies to Metaphysics the dignity of a science of realities.

There are present then, concreted in an individual object of sense-experience two kinds of modes or aspects of reality. One set of those objective modes of reality are formally and intuitively perceived by sense, and another set of those modes of reality are formally perceived by intellect alone, such as "substance" for example. Both sense and intellect perceive the first set, the senses in the *concrete*, the intellect in the *abstract*, as for example, color, extension, motion, etc., that is, all the "proper" and "common" objects of sense are perceived in these twofold ways. But it is only the intellect can perceive, as its own proper objects, the modes of reality of the second set. Is it not reasonable to expect, that the intellect and the senses, so totally different as faculties in their natures, should have their own proper objects in the "material object" of sense-experience? Is it not reasonable also, that the aspects of reality perceived by the superior faculty of intellect, be as objectively real as the aspects of reality perceived by the inferior faculties of sense?

Now Locke admits that he possesses the intellectual ideas of "substance," "cause," "necessity," etc., which he realizes cannot be derived *directly* either through the channel of external "sensation" or through the channel of "reflection," and which to Locke is "properly an internal sense." The simple reason is that "substance," "cause," "necessity" are neither "proper," which Locke calls "secondary," nor "common," which Locke calls "primary," objects of sense. No sense, external or internal, is capable of perceiving directly and "per se" "substance," "cause," "necessity," etc.

How does Locke account for the presence of those intellectual ideas in his mind? Without scruple or apology, he forthwith abandons his previously asserted theory, that all his original ideas are derived through the sensuous channels of "sensation" and "reflection," and in his desperation to advance some other theory for their origin, dogmatically and gratuitously asserts, as we have seen, that the idea of "substance" "is nothing but the *supposed, unknown* support of those qualities we find existing, which we *imagine* cannot subsist without something to support them." That is, "substance," according to Locke's gratuitous solution of its origin, is only a "supposition" of the mind, and, therefore, is but a fatuous phantom projected from out the mind. Substance is then a pure *creation of the mind*. No wonder Locke said, "substance" is an objective reality "unknown." Of course, as an actual existence in objects, it is "unknown" to Locke, firstly because he confesses it was never derived as a mode of reality from existing objects, since it came from a "supposition" of the mind, and secondly because whatever Locke knows, he knows by sense-faculties, and "substance" does not *per se* affect sense.

When Locke says that we "imagine that qualities cannot subsist without something to support them," the implication is that we are mistaken in thinking that "qualities" always *qualify* something, and therefore, we are rationally obliged to correct the mistake, and assert, that *qualities as such*, can and do exist *in* and *through* themselves, and are therefore "substances." "If you throw reason out by the door, it will come back by the window." Without committing intellectual suicide men cannot get rid of "substance." A quality necessarily imports a qualified. The fundamental reason why Locke says "we have no clear idea of substance" is, because as a Sensist he could not form a sensuous or picturable idea of substance. He seems to forget that we are not mere animals and that we can clearly understand what we cannot picture.

Let us now examine Locke's account of the origin of the idea of "cause." He seems to be timorous in assigning to it an origin. Because cause cannot again be derived from either of his two sensuous channels of sense-experience, sensation and reflection, so he again invents the following origin of the idea of "cause." He says: "So also finding that the substance, wood, which is a certain collection of simple ideas *so-called,* by the application of fire, is turned into another substance called ashes; that is another complex idea, consisting of a collection of simple ideas, quite different from that complex idea which we call wood; we *consider* fire, in relation to ashes, as cause, and the ashes, as effect. So that whatever is considered by us to conduce or operate to the producing of any particular idea or collection of simple ideas, whether substance or mode, which did not before exist, *hath thereby in our minds* the relation of cause, and so is denominated by us." (B. II. XXVI. 1.) (*Scoring ours.*)

On this passage we make the following reflections. If the "idea of cause" is a direct object of sense, as Locke maintains, there can be found no idea in the adequate comprehension of cause, except what can be perceived by the senses. What are the senses capable of perceiving in what we commonly call cause? They can perceive for example "the fire," that is, "a body on fire" as the *antecedent* to the "ashes," and the "ashes" as a *consequent.* But sense can perceive this antecedent and this consequent only as isolated, *unrelated* facts. To perceive a universal "relation," between antecedents and consequents, which we call a "cause," is absolutely beyond the perceptive power of any sense. Because a universal and necessary "relation" is not an object *per se* of any sense, a dog cannot perceive such a "relation." If he could he would make use of fire, I am afraid, to cause considerable damage when aroused to anger. Universal and necessary "relation" is an object of intellect only.

Moreover, there is enfolded in cause more of content than is expressed by antecedent and consequent. There is also involved in the comprehension of the idea of cause a necessary and universal relation, and in addition, the idea of origination and efficient production of something that begins to be. We challenge Locke, or any Sensist to show that "the relation of cause has its rise from ideas received from sensation or reflection," that is, received from the senses. What sense external or internal, has for its object "necessity," "universality," "origination," and "efficiency?" A cat can look at a king, but it could never know that he is a king. In like manner senses can perceive *what is* de facto a cause, but no sense can perceive that *it is a cause*, because the ideas that cause involves, as we have explained, cannot be *per se* perceived by the exercise of any sense.

Locke, then, literally "bootlegs" into his idea of a "cause," purely intellectual notions, despite his previously declared law, that all ideas arise in the mind through the double sense-experience sources of "sensation" and "reflection" and then deceives himself by not considering those intellectual notions as contraband smuggled into his theory of Sensism.

Since the idea of cause could not be derived, then, from any sense or combination of senses, how did Locke explain its origin? His explanation seems contradictory. In one passage he says—"the notion of cause and effect has its rise from ideas received by sensation and reflection," (B. II. XXVI. 2) and in the passage already quoted (B. II. XXVI. 1) he says—"so that whatever is considered by us to conduce or operate to the producing of any particular simple idea, or collection of ideas, whether substance or mode (accident) which did not before exist, hath thereby *in our minds* the relation of cause, and is so denominated by us." (Italics ours.) The phrase "hath thereby in our minds the relation of cause" can have no other meaning, and that, too, without offering any violence to the text, except that cause as a relation is something *purely mental* and *subjective* generated by the mind itself. Locke does not say that the relation of cause exists between objects external to, and independent of the mind, because he knows as a sensuous phenomenalist no such objects; but says, that whatever we *consider* as producing something else, (he does not say "whatever produces something else") "hath thereby *in our minds* the relation of cause." This means that the idea of cause like the idea of substance has its origin in the mind itself and hence is a product or pure creation of the mind. It is true that Locke somewhat camouflages the origin of the idea of cause by vague expression. No wonder that Hume, whose philosophy is only the logical development of Locke's teaching, subsequently tore rudely away the vague camouflage of Locke, and honest Sensist as he was, bluntly asserted that cause has its origin in mere "*custom*," and is not grounded on objective existence at all.

Locke also admitted that he possessed the idea of "necessity." He says for instance: "Hence, when we talk or think of any particular sort of substance as horse, stone, etc., though the idea we have of either of them be but the *complication or collection of those several simple ideas of sensible qualities,* which we used to find united in a thing called horse or stone, yet, *because we cannot conceive how they should subsist alone, nor one in another,* we *suppose* them existing in, and supported by, some common subject, which support we denote by the name substance." (B. II. XXIII. 4.)

We wish to make use of the testimony set forth in this quotation to establish this one point only, to wit, that Locke admitted that he possessed the idea of necessity. "We cannot conceive" he says, "how they (qualities) should subsist alone." That is, we *must* think that our minds are *necessitated,* obliged to think, that qualities cannot stand alone, but that qualities *must* by their nature *qualify something.* Locke here recognizes the idea of necessity.

Again Locke writes: "In the next place, man knows by an intuitive certainty, that *bare nothing can no more produce any real being, than it can be equal to two right angles.* . . . If, therefore, we know there is some real being it is an evident demonstration, that *from eternity there has been something;* since what was not from eternity had a beginning; and what had a beginning must be produced by something else." (B. IV. X. 3.)

This passage, though its consistency with the definition of knowledge given previously by Locke may be challenged, testifies at least, that Locke acknowledged the possession of the idea of "necessity." "What had a beginning," he says, "*must* be produced by something else." "Must" implies "necessity" in his idea of cause.

Now we ask whence came this idea of "necessity." It certainly could not come to him through the senses alone. "Necessity" is not a direct object *per se* of any external or internal sense. It is obviously not an "idea of sensation" nor an "idea of reflection," because "reflection" for Locke is "properly an internal sense." Even if we admit that Locke was legitimately and logically a Realist as he professes to be, still his senses, through which he professes to acquire all his ideas, could tell him at best what *is* in particular cases, never what *must be* in every case. The truth is that the "idea of necessity" is a supersensible, intellectual idea just as the ideas of "substance" and "cause." Those ideas, "substance," "cause," "necessity," are not ideas derived from experience by the senses. The simple reason is that they do not, and cannot *per se* directly *affect* the senses. Were we endowed only by sense faculties, we would never possess those ideas. A dog can, indeed, perceive by his senses or sight *what is a substance,* and *what is a cause,* but the dog could never know that *it is a substance,* and *it is a cause.* Scholasticism expresses this last truth by saying that substance and cause are objects "per accidens" of sense. They are objective in an existing object of experience; they are contained objectively in experience, but they cannot be discovered in that experience by the senses alone. They are discovered in an object of experience only by the higher faculty of intellect. We can apprehend by intellect what, in experience, the senses cannot *per se* perceive.

Hence it follows that all ideas, which Locke has recognized as the possession of man, are not "ideas of sensation" and "ideas of reflection," Locke to the contrary notwithstanding. Yet strange to say, Locke failed to modify his hypothesis of Sensism to harmonize with the fact that he admitted ideas that the senses never conveyed to his mind. And since he could not derive these ideas either through "sensation" or "reflection," the sources of all ideas that for him represent objective reality, he explained their origin as subjective creations produced by the generative power of the mind which do not reveal any objective reality.

Locke also attempted but failed, to explain the origin of "infinity" and "eternity" from the point of view of Sensism. He admitted that he possessed those ideas. He professed to have come by them through "sensation and reflection." He says, "It suffices in my design to show . . . how even the idea we have of infinity, how remote soever it may seem to be from any object of sense, or operation of our mind, has, nevertheless, as all our other ideas, its origin there," i.e., "from sensation and reflection." (B. II. XVII. 22.)

If Locke meant by this statement that "the idea of infinity" had its origin in sense-knowledge (sensation and reflection) and understood by "origin" that the initial knowledge of a nucleus of some very limited perfection had its rise in sense-experience, and that afterwards that very limited perfection was elaborated by intellect through (1) abstraction, (2) the removal of all limits, and (3) by the employment of analogy, Locke would be right. For all knowledge *begins* in sense-experience. But if he means, as he seems to mean, that the idea of infinity is acquired by the mere endless increase of the very finite nucleus of perfection positively given in sense, he is certainly wrong. For the mere endless, progressive repetition of finites could never result in the infinite. Even endless additions of finites would still be finite.

Yet Locke explicitly states, inveterate Sensist as he is, that the idea of infinity is acquired by this endless increase of what is finite.

He writes: "Everyone that has any idea of any stated lengths of space, as a foot, finds that he can repeat that idea; and joining it to the former, make an idea of two feet; and by the addition of a third, three feet; and so on,

without ever coming to an end of his additions, whether
of the same idea of a foot, or, if he pleases, of doubling it,
or any other idea he has of any length, as a mile, or
diameter of the earth. . . . For, whichsoever of these he
takes, and how often soever he doubles, or otherwise mul-
tiplies it, he finds that, after he has continued his doub-
lings in his thoughts, and enlarged his idea as much as
he pleases, he has no more reason to stop, nor is one jot
nearer to the end of his addition, than he was at the first
setting out; the power of his enlarging his idea of space
by further additions remaining still the same, he hence
takes the idea of infinite space," (B. II. XXVII. 3.)

This crude, sensuous, spatio-morphic method of explaining the origin of the idea of infinite space or spatial
immensity is an attempt to explain the impossible. Infinite space as an actual reality is an impossibility, because that is not infinite which can be added to or sub-
tracted from. The illusion of infinite space has its origin
in the false assumption that *imagines* (spatium imagin-
arium) that space considered in the *abstract actually
exists* as a void which bodies fill. Such imaginary space
is a fiction. Cf. Joyce, Natural Theology, p. 325.

Locke's account for the origin of the idea of "eternity"
proceeds in the same puerile, sensuous manner. He attempts to encompass the idea of eternity by a progressive
addition of finite portions of time. He says: "By the same
means, therefore, and from the same original that we
come to have the idea of time, we have also that idea
which we call eternity; viz., having got the idea of succession and duration, by reflecting on the train of our own
ideas, caused in us either by the natural appearances of
those ideas coming constantly of themselves into our
waking thoughts, or else caused by external objects suc-
cessively affecting our senses; and having from the revolution of the sun got the ideas of certain lengths of duration, we can in our thoughts *add such lengths of duration
to one another,* as often as we please, and apply them, so
added, to durations past and to come. And this can con-

tinue to go on, without bounds or limits and proceed *ad infinitum.*" (B. II. XIV. 27.)

It is obvious again that no number of progressive additions of finite lengths of time will engender the idea of eternity. The sum of such additions will still be finite. Leibnitz's criticism of the above passage of Locke may be illuminating. Leibnitz writes: "But in order to draw from them (the added lengths of time) the notion of *eternity,* it is necessary to think besides that the same reason always exists for going farther. It is this *rational consideration* which achieves the notion of the infinite (in duration). *Thus the senses alone cannot suffice* to cause the formation of those notions." Critique of Locke, p. 158.

We shall now finish our study of Locke by indicating a few other doctrines characteristic of his teaching.

Following Descartes he taught that, what he called the "secondary qualities" of bodies, which for Scholasticism are the "proper objects" of the external senses, such as color, sound, etc., do not exist *"formally"* in external, material objects, but only "causally" that is, external objects cause in our organic external senses the phenomena which Locke calls "secondary qualities" and Scholasticism the "proper objects" of the external senses. If, for example, a tree should fall in the forest, where no ear of man or beast is present to hear the crashing sound of the falling tree, then, no sound "formally" as sound, would exist. The falling tree would have the power of producing sound in an ear, were it present. The sound, therefore, formally considered, would be in the ear, not an actually existing phenomenon outside and independent of an ear, whether an ear was present to hear, or not. Taste, color, odor, resistance, Locke would explain in the same manner.

Only those qualities which Locke calls "primary" and Scholasticism terms "common objects of sense" actually exist "formally" in external, material objects, assuming that Locke could know those external objects. Such qualities are, for instance, extension, motion, etc.

Another characteristic doctrine of Locke is, that matter may be conceived as capable of thinking. Locke sets forth this doctrine, thus: "We have the ideas of *matter* and *thinking*, but possibly shall never be able to know whether any mere material being thinks or not; it being impossible for us, by the contemplation of our own ideas, without revelation, to discover whether omnipotency has not given to some systems of nature, fitly disposed, a power to perceive, and think....... It being, in respect to our notions, not much more remote from our comprehension to conceive that God can, if He pleases, superadd to matter *a faculty of thinking*, than that He should superadd to it another substance *with a faculty of thinking*. For I see no contradiction in it, that the first Eternal, thinking Being, or Omnipotent Spirit, should if He pleased, give to certain systems of created senseless matter, put together as He thinks fit, some degrees of sense, perception, and thought."   (B. IV. III. 6.)   Locke, therefore, asserts the possibility at least, that it is a material substance that thinks in us.   This expressed opinion of Locke opened the door to the Materialism of the eighteenth and subsequent centuries in England, France and the United States.

Locke's argument to establish his materialistic theory is grounded on a false principle.   We cannot discover by natural reason, he claims, whether God has not given to some mere material substances, fitly disposed, the power to perceive and think, because forsooth we have no comprehensive or exhaustive knowledge of the power of matter.   We reply, that it is not necessary to know everything about matter to arrive at a certain judgment of what matter cannot do.   We know that "you cannot gather grapes from thistles or figs from thorns," yet no scientist has an exhaustive knowledge of the matter that constitutes those plants.   The properties of matter which we do know, make manifest to us its essential nature. All men, even Locke himself, argue legitimately and with certainty from the known properties of things to their nature.   Hence we can conclude with certain evidence, that the properties of intellectual thought revealed to us by consciousness, are diametrically opposed to the properties which experience reveals to us in matter, and that, consequently, those two sets of properties cannot co-exist in the same substance. God, therefore, could not dispose matter to think any more than He could make a square circle.

CHAPTER VI

GEORGE BERKELEY, IRISH IDEALIST*

GEORGE BERKELEY was undoubtedly the keenest, freshest, most original thinker in the history of English philosophy. Even in the charm of his style, he is unsurpassed by any English philosophical writer. This has been the verdict of his contemporaries; present-day critics have corroborated that judgment. "To Berkeley every virtue under heaven." Thus did Alexander Pope, charmed by his unaffected virtues and brilliant genius, sing of George Berkeley, the Irish Idealist. Few men of any age who had the temerity to contradict the accepted convictions of their times, have won such unanimous admiration from their critical contemporaries as did Berkeley. Not only did the satirical pen of Pope praise him, the acidity of Dean Swift sweeten in his presence, and Addison love him, but the callous Prime Minister, Walpole and his parliament were impressed by him, even the phlegmatic George I was roused to take an interest in his schemes and the turbulent Bishop Otterbury could say of him: "So much learning, so much knowledge, so much innocence, and such humility, I did not think had been the portion of any but angels, till I saw this gentleman." Professor Morris, late of Johns Hopkins, Baltimore, and the translator of Ueberweg, ends a brief sketch of Berkeley's life by this eulogy:—"The truest, acutest philosopher, that Great Britain (sic) has ever known."

Yet strange to say, though Berkeley was one of Ireland's most distinguished sons, he is almost forgotten by his countrymen. Fronting Trinity College, Dublin, Berkeley's Alma Mater, and his home as student and Fellow for twenty years, are erected magnificent statues to Edmund Burke and Oliver Goldsmith. But the Protestants of Ireland never thought of perpetuating in bronze,

---

* Reprinted from "Thought" (June, 1926), with the kind permission of The Editor.

at their great seat of learning, the memory of George
Berkeley. This neglect may be easily explained. An intensely Catholic community could not be expected to remember a Protestant Bishop whom his co-religionists had
forgotten. The Low Church Irish Protestants had no
love for Berkeley. In temper and affection for his countrymen, he seems to glory, not in the conceit of hyphena-
tion, but in being a plain, unappended Irishman. I quote
the following passages from his "Common Place Book,"
not for the opinions they express, but for the frank Irish-
ism they profess. He says:—

"There are men who say there are insensible exten-
sions. There are others who say the wall is not white,
the iron is not hot, etc. We Irishmen cannot attain to
these truths."

"The mathematicians think there are insensible lines.
About these they harangue. We Irishmen can conceive
no such lines."

"The mathematicians talk of what they call a point.
This, they say, is not altogether nothing, nor is it down-
right something. Now we *Irishmen* are apt to think
something (in the abstract) and nothing are next neighbors." Speaking of the publication of one of his books
he remarks: "I publish not this so much for anything else
than to know whether other men have the same ideas as
we *Irishmen*." He was thoroughly Irish in insensibly in-
gratiating himself into the minds of others by the exercise
of that persuasive power, which his country-men call
"palaver" or "blarney." He says: "He that would bring
another over to his opinions, must seem to harmonize with
him at first, and humor him in his own way of talking."

This treading on the toes of established prejudice did
not help Berkeley to win the good graces of Irish Pres-
byterians or Irish low Church reactionaries. Their aloof-
ness from Berkeley was the penalty of his originality.
When not oppressed, when in the enjoyment of its free
activities, the Irish mind, as history testifies, is not commercial or world-shackled, but intensely and congenitally
intellectual. And no doubt when modern Ireland comes

into its own, it will recognize Berkeley for what was noble in him.

Berkeley's interest to me, lies not in his philosophical doctrines, though the winged flights of his Idealism were, at least nobler and more refined, than the grovelling Sensism of Locke and the Materialism which was its outcome. His interest lies in this, that he was in his thought, and as far as a Protestant could be, a symbol of his country, and a type of the Irish mind.

Whether it is a natural gift of Heaven, or a luxurious overgrowth of their Faith, or whether it is an effect upon their temperament of the multiplicity of natural beauties concentrated in so small a bit of earth as Ireland, beauties heightened by a climate as soft as a mother's smile, without being languid or depressing, the Irish people have a proverbial facility for sensing and visualizing the spiritual, the supersensible and the ideal. The spirit and the things of the spirit are more real to them, than matter and the things of matter. The visible is the invisible, and the unseen is the seen. Their super-vision, or as the Irish call it, their "second sight" pushes aside the clayey mounds of old Danish forts, or peers through the crumbling battlements of ruined castles, illumines with a thousand lights the forgotten banquet hall, and in wonderment gazes at the enthroned queen of Fairyland attended by gallant chiefs in shining armor, and grand ladies bedecked with other-world beauty.

We wonder not that Ireland, comforting herself with the vision of the unseen during the grim Penal years of the 17th and the 18th centuries and breathing an idealistic atmosphere such as this, should have produced a Berkeley. The philosophy of a people is the expression of their deeply seated tendencies.

The machine-like and orderly precision of the French mind gave us Descartes, who attempted to reason out geometrically the remotest conclusions of his system after the manner of mathematics from a single central principle, "I think, therefore I exist." Locke gave philosophical expression to the sensistic and materialistic tendencies of the English mind. The practical "get-there-spirit" of America produced the Pragmatism or Practicalism of William James. It is not surprising, then, that Ireland, which so easily envisages the unseen, should have had its counterpart in the Idealism of Berkeley. Berkeley is, in his way, a symbol of Ireland, as Locke is a symbol of England, Descartes a symbol of France, and William James a symbol of America. Each, indeed, has given us a one-sided and exaggerated interpretation of the best thought of their respective countries. Still each remains the typical product of the tendencies that lie nearest to the heart of their race and people. When a Frenchman yields to his passion for precision and orderly centralization, his philosophy becomes a machine. When an Englishman loses his poise and balance, he falls into Materialism. When an American idolizes the mere practical and forgets the larger vision of other truths, he is naturally a Pragmatist. And so when an Irishman is captivated by the vision of the unseen to the neglect of all other phases of reality, he ignores this "too solid earth," and revels in the fairyland of the Ideal. He will take it as a mere trifle to suffer and even die for an ideal. Such was George Berkeley, the amiable Irish dreamer.

Who, then, was this extraordinary man?

I

George Berkeley was born near Thomastown, in the Co. of Kilkenny, March 12, 1685. He was the eldest of a family of six sons. Later on, the family must have removed to Tipperary. According to a record in Trinity College, one of George's brothers was born "near Thurles" in 1689. His father was Irish born, but of English descent. His mother was Irish both by birth and by blood, and is said to have been in some way related to General Wolfe, the hero of Quebec. The family was by no means wealthy. At George's birth, his father occupied the comparatively humble position of Custom-Officer. At the age of twelve George was sent to the Kilkenny school, then the Eton of Ireland, famous alike for its learned masters

and distinguished pupils.   Twenty years before, in this
school, the poet, Congreve, and Swift received their early
training.

At the age of fifteen, Berkeley entered Trinity College,
Dublin. During his undergraduate days, some pronounced
him a dunce, others a genius.   In 1704, the year of Locke's
death, he took his Bachelor's degree and three years later
became Master, and was admitted as a Fellow of the
College.   He was now twenty-two years of age, ardent,
ambitious, enthusiastic, deeply religious, wholly free from
selfishness, touched too, with the chivalry of a knight-
errant to strike a blow, not at Donnybrook Fair, but in the
bitter intellectual battles that then raged in France, England and Dublin, as the aftermath of Descartes' rationalism, Locke's materialistic and Tillotson's deistic free-
thinking.

To understand Berkeley's philosophical system, we
must here break the narrative of his life, and take a brief
survey of the new and destructive forces of thought, to
counteract which, Berkeley bent all the genius of his
Idealistic temperament.   Just as in our time, the shock
of the great war has left the economical and political balance of the nations turning restlessly on its bases, so that
no man can tell whether it will ultimately come to rest in
oppression or in freedom, so at the beginning of the
eighteenth century, when Berkeley donned his Master's
gown, all the great truths vital to humanity,—God, the
soul, the existence of the material world, Christianity
itself, were so obscured and confused by the leaders of
thought, that where these truths were not denied outright, they were at least seriously doubted.   Scepticism
and Atheism and Deism were swinging their axes at the
root principles of all the fundamental truths vital to
humanity. The fundamental truth of all times, is of
course, the existence of a Personal God outside and independent of the universe He has created.   It is the root
principle of all religion.   The vigorous words of St.
Augustine remain forever true—"Justice cannot exist
without religion, nor religion without God."   And "without

justice, states are nothing else than bands of robbers, as bands of robbers are nothing else but little states." (City of God, IV. 4.) In France, Cartesianism through the rationalistic tendencies of Descartes, the Occasionalism of Geulincx and the Ontologism of Malebranche had ended in Pantheism in the philosophy of Spinoza. Pantheism is only another name for Atheism masquerading in the respectable garb of a philosophical system. This new enlightenment of France and the Continent, found its way into all the great seats of learning of the time, and Protestant Trinity College, Dublin, during Berkeley's undergraduate days, was not proof against its invasion.

Another stream of "new thought," having its origin in England and Ireland, met the French and Continental stream, in Berkeley's youth, and both uniting in a stronger current, threatened to achieve the same purpose of destroying the truth of God's existence. The influence of John Locke's crude and illogical Sensism was at its height when Berkeley was a Fellow of Trinity. This Sensism of Locke was materialistic in its tendencies. Nor was Locke wanting in disciples who quickly developed the materialism latent in his system. Only three years after Berkeley had received his degree of Master, Toland, an Irishman, published his "Pantheisticon" (1710), wherein he taught that matter was eternal, that, not only all changes in the world without us, but all thought can be ultimately resolved into mechanical motion, that the Deity is one with Nature or the material universe, thereby denying a transcedent God. Toland went so far as to institute a new pantheistic religion, "in which science was to be the new scripture, and men of science the new priesthood and the future educators of humanity."

Toland's Pantheism was indeed censured by the Irish Parliament, burned by the common hangman, denounced by every Protestant pulpit in the land, and the author himself forced to leave the country. But ideas will not burn, nor can you stab them to death by a bayonet-point. Error can be overcome only by truth, and wrong by justice. Even colonial America did not escape this wave of

Materialism. It was vigorously propagated here by the writings and influence of Cadwallader Colden, (1688-1776), an Irish medical doctor who first settled in Philadelphia, afterwards in New York, where he gave up the practice of medicine, and became in succession, during the years immediately preceding the Revolution, Surveyor General, Master in Chancery, Member of the Council, and Lieutenant Governor of the province of New York. He finally settled at Coldenham near Albany, then, as he himself has said, "the home of wolves and bears and other wild animals." It is curious to note, that it was among the Cavaliers of the South rather than among the Puritans of the North, that Materialism, just before the Revolution, had been very widely adopted. Philadelphia was its propagating center, and Priestly, with Benjamin Rush of that city and Joseph Buchanan of Kentucky its leading apostles.

It was into this welter of Materialism that denied the soul, and of Pantheism that denied a Personal God, and of Deism that flouted the supernatural in Christianity, that George Berkeley, at the age of twenty-two, almost a boy, without wealth, prestige, or the influence of personal friends, was thrust, either to swim onward ingloriously with its current, or conceive the high resolve of stemming it, with the only resources within his power—his philosophical genius, and the charm of a literary style. By those who yet believe, as I believe, that next to God's help, the factor that decides a noble choice in critical moments of young lives, is the naturally good instincts and temperament which we have inherited from a long line of highly moral ancestors, it cannot be doubted that it was the blood and character of his mother that spoke in the son, when George Berkeley flung down his gauntlet and determined to consecrate his life to do battle against sordid Materialism, deified Pantheism, and rationalising Deism, because he conceived that those three "isms" are the deadliest enemies of humanity.

In 1709, the year before he published his "Principles," he was ordained deacon in the chapel of Trinity College,

Dublin. His one reliable friend at this time was Sir John Percival, who afterwards became the Earl of Egmont. Sir John Percival was then in London. Berkeley was anxious to know what reception his new ideas, embodied in his late book, "The Principles of Knowledge," received from the learned world of England. Writing to Sir John Percival, he received from him the following answer:

"I did but name the subject matter of your book of "Principles" to some ingenious friends of mine, and they immediately treated it with ridicule, at the same time refusing to read it; which I have not yet got one to do. A physician of my acquaintance undertook to describe your person, and argued you must needs be mad, and that you ought to take remedies. A Bishop pitied you, that a desire and vanity of starting something new, should put you upon such an undertaking; and when I justified you on that part of your character and added other deserving qualities you have, he could not tell what to think of you. Another told me an ingenious man ought to be discouraged from his wit; but that you are not gone so far as a gentleman in town, who asserts that there is not only no such thing as matter, but that we ourselves have no being at all."

Pope, who admired Berkeley, characterized this kind of criticism in the satirical line:

"Coxcombs vanquish Berkeley with a grin."

The sense of a noble cause, backed by youth, ardor and ambition in the Idealist of Trinity College, was only stimulated to new efforts by being ridiculed and called "a madman." The two years following the publication of his "Principles," Berkeley spent in preparing to reproduce his idealistic conception of the universe in the dramatic form of dialogue. So he published in 1713 his three dialogues between "Hylas and Philonous." As a piece of philosophical literature, this work stands even today, unrivaled and unsurpassed in the history of the English language. The exquisite felicity of its style, the precision of its language, the lucidity of its thought, and the warmth of its sympathy make it a unique gem in the crown of Anglo-Irish literature. And yet this gem is the work of a young Irishman, twenty-seven years of age, who up to this time had received all his education within the shores of his own sea-girt island. The work itself is a Socratic conversation on the new doctrine between Philonous—Berkeley himself, and the educated man in the street, represented by Hylas.

Berkeley, on January 1713, while the dialogues between Hylas and Philonous were in press, visited London for the first time. He was now twenty-seven.

II

The personal charm of the young Irish Plato immediately dissolved the reputation of "madman" which preceded him; and the inconsiderate ridicule of the cynics, who knew neither the man nor his writings, was quickly changed into unaffected admiration and friendly interest, on the part of the literary celebrities of the time in London. He dined frequently with his countryman Steele; he was the guest of Addison to witness the first presentation of the great essayist's play, "Cato"; Alexander Pope was captivated by him; Dean Swift, then in London, presented him at Court, recommended him to all the Ministers of State, and promised him favor. He was an honored visitor at Oxford. The literary energy of the youthful Berkeley was untiring. During his brief stay in London he contributed four papers to the "Guardian."

The scene of Berkeley's life now changes. In October (1713) as Chaplain to Lord Peterborough, he visited France, Italy, and Sicily. Berkeley met Malebranche in Paris. A mythical story invented by wags, tells that Berkeley during the visit, was the innocent occasion of Malebranche's death. The conversation of the first philosopher of Great Britain and Ireland and of the first philosopher of France, naturally turned on their respective systems. In the heat of the debate, the story goes, Malebranche, yielding to the impetuosity of his Gallic nature, raised his voice so high, that he brought on a violent attack of his disorder, which carried him off in a few days.

On his return from the continent, Berkeley expected a living at St. Paul's Cathedral, London. But the politicians balked his appointment, because they suspected him of Jacobitism. Instead, the Protestant Bishop of Clogher engaged him as a traveling tutor to his son. Berkeley enjoyed traveling. He pushed his way over the Alps, sauntered through the Italian cities, visited Rome, and basked on the sunny shores of Sicily. A contemporary writer gives us an interesting sketch of his restless desire for knowledge at this time. He says:

"This very great—though singular kind of man, begrudged neither pain nor expense for the means of information. He travelled through a great part of Sicily on foot, clambered over the mountains and crept into the caverns, to discover its natural history and discover the causes of its volcanoes, and I have known him to sit for hours in forges and foundries to inspect their successive operations."

On his way home from Italy the dominating purpose of his life at this time, namely to strike a blow at Materialism and Atheism, expressed itself in an essay on "Motion" written in Latin.

In 1721, Berkeley was back in London. The generous motto of his life "non sibi sed toti mundo," was at this period, giving birth in his mind to a vision of one of those extraordinary projects, that, in zeal and unselfish devotion to humanity, rivaled the zealous enterprises of his countrymen, when Irishmen were the apostles and educators of Europe. He deliberately made up his mind to shake the dust of England from his feet, and turn his hopes beyond the Atlantic, there to spend the rest of his life in educating and civilizing the savage Indians of the American forests, and the unfortunate negro slaves of the English colonial plantations. In 1723 he opened his heart to his friend, Sir John Percival, in the following letter:

"It is now about ten months since I have determined to spend the residue of my days in Bermuda, where I trust in Providence, I may be the mean in-

strument of doing great good to mankind—whatever
happens, go I am resolved, if I live. Half a dozen of
the most ingenious and agreeable men in our college
are with me in this project, and since I came thither
(to London), I have got together about a dozen
Englishmen of quality who intend to retire to these
islands."

So enthusiastic an appeal did this missionary life make
to Berkeley's whole nature, that he gave expression to it
in a poem entitled "Verses on the Prospect of Planting
Arts and Learning in America," some lines of which have
won immortality. I quote a few stanzas—

The Muse, disgusted at an age and clime
    Barren of every glorious theme,
In distant lands, now waits a better time
    Producing subjects worthy fame:

There, shall be sung another golden age,
    The rise of Empire and of Arts,
The good and great inspiring epic rage
    The wisest heads and noblest hearts.

Not such as Europe breeds in her decay;
    Such as she bred when fresh and young,
When heavenly flame did animate her clay
    By future poets shall be sung.

Westward the Course of Empire takes its way;
    The first four Acts already past,
A fifth shall close the Drama with the day;
    Time's noblest offspring is her last.

We must now briefly examine the trend of events in
England and Ireland that induced Berkeley to make the
supreme sacrifice of exile. Why did Berkeley despair of
England? Why was he disgusted with the "age and
clime?" Why did he look on Europe as decadent, and
England as effete and undone? It was in the days of the
South Sea Bubble—a gigantic commercial speculation,
founded on fraud. It ended in a failure which threw
England into misery and social agitation. Berkeley saw

in this catastrophe only a confirmation of his conviction, that England was politically corrupt, religiously decadent and irremediably immoral. To give expression to his indignation and zealous to save a remnant from the wreck of that religious instinct and reverence for morality, that made England great in the past, Berkeley wrote his famous "Essay towards Preventing the Ruin of Great Britain."

Listen to Berkeley, like a prophet of old, raising his voice, like a Banshee cry, bewailing the vanished piety of Great Britain:

"I know, it is an old folly to make peevish complaint of the time, and charge the common failures to human nature on a particular age. One may, nevertheless, venture to affirm, that the present hath brought forth new and portentous villainies, not to be paralleled in our own or any other history. We have been long preparing for such great catastrophe. Vice and villainy have, by degrees, grown reputable among us; our infidels have passed for fine gentlemen; and our venal traitors for men of sense, who knew the world. We have made a jest of public spirit and cancelled all respect for whatever our law and religion have reputed sacred. The old English modesty is quite worn off, and instead of blushing for our crimes, we are ashamed only of piety and virtue. In short other nations have been wicked but we are the first, who have been wicked upon principle."
(Essay)

What grounds had Berkeley for the indictment, which he expressed when he said, "Our infidels have passed for fine gentlemen." We call Bishop Butler, the author of the "Analogy," to bear witness—Butler was a contemporary of Berkeley. Bishop Butler, in the beginning of his "Analogy," writes:

"It is come, I know not how, taken for granted by many persons, that Christianity is not so much as a subject of enquiry, but it is now at length discovered to be fictitious. And accordingly they treat of it, as if in the present age, this was an agreed point of all people of discernment ("fine gentlemen") ; and nothing remained but to set it up as a principal subject of mirth and ridicule. We have cancelled all respect for what religion reputes sacred—for having so long interrupted the pleasures of the world."

Such was the England of the eighteenth century which the moral temperament of Berkeley repudiated, to find amidst the untutored savages of America, a more congenial field for his energy and zeal. Historians may deem Berkeley's views of eighteenth century England exaggerated. We are only interested, with the view of explaining Berkeley's attitude of mind, that such were his views.

We have now seen, from the evidence of a contemporary witness, why Berkeley was

> Disgusted at an age and clime
> Barren of every glorious theme,

and why he determined to make the supreme resolve of exiling himself among the aborigines of America. Yet before he could carry out his purpose many difficulties confronted him.

He had to beg for funds from friendly sympathizers, procure a charter and government support for his college. In the meantime he was appointed to one of the best livings in Ireland—the deanery of Derry, which brought him as salary the handsome sum of 5,500 pounds sterling a year. Yet to carry out his project, he with remarkable detachment from ease and position, surrendered this lucrative position as if it were a mere trifle. His feelings at this time are well revealed by Dean Swift, in a letter to the Lord Lieutenant of Ireland, recommending to him his friend Berkeley. Amongst other things the Dean writes characteristically:

"I am now to mention his (Berkeley's) errand. He is an absolute philosopher with regard to money, titles, and power; and for three years past has been struck with a notion of founding a university in the Bermudas. . . . He showed me a little tract, which he designs to publish, and there your excellency will see his whole scheme of a

college founded for Indian scholars and missionaries;
where he most exorbitantly proposes a whole $500 a year
for himself, $250 for a Fellow, and $50 for a student. His
heart will break if his deanery be not taken from him,
and left to your Excellency's disposal. I discouraged him
by the coldness of Courts and Ministers, who will interpret all this, as impossible and a vision; but nothing will
do. And, therefore, I humbly entreat your Excellency,
either to use such persuasions as will keep one of the first
men of the Kingdom for learning and virtue at home, or
assist him by your credit to compass his romantic design."

In the tract which he published, to advertise and col-
lect funds for his College in Bermuda, Berkeley speaks
in no flattering terms of the English colonists in America.
He calls them "avaricious, licentious and irreligious," and
cleverly touches the danger to England of Roman Catholic ascendency in America, saying:

"In Europe the Protestant Religion hath of late
considerably lost ground, and America seems the
likeliest place where to make up what hath been lost
in Europe, provided the proper means be taken.
Otherwise the Spanish missionaries in the South and
the French in the North, are making such a progress,
as may one day spread the religion of Rome, and
with it the usual hatred of Protestants, throughout
all the savage nations of America, which would prob-
ably end in the extirpation of our Colonies, on the
safety whereof depends so much of the nation's
wealth, and so considerable a branch of his Majesty's
revenue."

He instinctively felt the secret of the Catholic missionaries' strength, when contrasted with Protestant
methods. He says: "It cannot be denied, that the great
number of poor regulars, inured to hard living, and
brought up in an implicit obedience to their superiors,
hath hitherto given the Church of Rome, in regard to her
missions, great advantages over the reformed Churches."
He here hints at the success of St. Francis Xavier in
India, whom his friend Percival urged him to rival. Ber-

keley succeeded in obtaining in 1726 a charter for his Bermuda College and a promise of 20,000 pounds from the House of Commons. The money was never paid.

In August, 1728, Berkeley took for his bride Anne Foster, daughter of the Speaker of the Irish House of Commons. She was a devout religious mystic, ready to share his fortune, when he was about to engage in one of the most romantic missionary enterprises of Protestants. "I chose her," he writes Sir John Percival, "for her qualities of mind and her unaffected inclination to books. She goes with great thankfulness, to live a plain farmer's wife, and wear stuff of her own spinning. I have presented her with a spinning wheel." She was a brave woman.

III

It was now September 5, 1728. Berkeley was in his forty-fourth year. Swinging at anchor at Gravesend, England, was a little boat of 250 tons, which the party had hired. In a letter to a friend, Berkeley writes these simple but thrilling words, expressive indeed of the highest mark of sacrifice to which Protestantism of all times has reached though still genuinely Protestant—a goodly measure of this world's comforts with a little dash of other-worldliness to give it dignity. He says: "Tomorrow with God's blessing, I set sail for Rhode Island with my wife and a friend of hers, my Lady Hancock's daughter, who bears us company. I am married, since I saw you, to Miss Foster, whose humor and turn of mind pleases me beyond anything I knew in her sex. Mr. James, Mr. Dalton, and Mr. Smibert go with us on the voyage," three out of the original eighteen volunteers. They carried stores and goods to a great value. Berkeley embarked 20,000 books, besides what the other gentlemen carried. The little bark tossed about the ocean for five months, and landed in Narragansett Bay, January 1729.

When George Berkeley with his little party stepped on board the nameless craft of 250 tons, at Gravesend, the cherished visions of his romantic life had, like the mid-day sun, reached the zenith of his hopefulness. That moment was the high noon of Berkeley's greatness.

When he stepped on the shore of Rhode Island five months later with his young wife, the glamor of the ever increasing brilliancy of his former career, began gradually, but steadily to decline. The world, alas, judges a man not by his visions, or good intentions, however noble, but by his achievements. And we search in vain for any palpable results to show, that Berkeley pushed his projected scheme into action, during his three years of sojourn in Rhode Island. He spent these years in a waiting inactivity. To blame Berkeley for this inactivity, however, which was painfully forced upon him, would be far from fair.

The House of Commons had enthusiastically voted him a grant of 20,000 pounds for the founding of his Bermuda College. Prime Minister Walpole promised to forward the money. Month after month passed and Walpole's promise was still unfulfilled. Berkeley, in a letter to Sir John Percival, March, 1730, speaks of his painful disappointment. He writes:

"I wait here with all the anxiety that attends suspense, until I know what I can depend upon, or what course I am to take. On the one hand I have no notion that the court would put what men call a bite upon a poor clergyman, who depended upon charters, grants, votes and the like engagements. On the other hand, I see nothing done towards the payment of the money. As for the raillery of European wits, I should not mind it, if I saw my College go on and prosper; but I must own the disappointments I have met with, in this particular, have nearly touched me, not without affecting my health and spirits. And, if after all that encouragement, they who engaged to endow and protect it (the college) let it drop, the disappointment indeed may be to me, but the censure I think will light elsewhere."

Berkeley stigmatizes Walpole, in these rapier words, with treachery, and the perfidy of a broken promise solemnly avowed.

No more striking embodiments of the irreconcilable difference between a Utilitarian and Materialistic civilization and an Idealistic and Spiritualistic one, could be presented to the gaze, than Prime Minister Walpole *in power* at home, and Berkeley *suffering* in exile. A paltry 20,000 pounds could then have planted in our southern States an infant college, that would have, in the course of years, undoubtedly developed into a University, that would perhaps today rival in greatness, Harvard, Yale, Princeton and Dartmouth. In intellectual reach and educational equipment the first presidents of these colleges could not compare with Berkeley, then one of the first men of Europe. The prestige of a great name has a wonderful influence, in creating in a seat of learning an intellectual atmosphere. I may be mistaken in thinking, but it seems, that the present University of Virginia, the only considerable center of learning in the South, does not measure up either in the reputation for scholarship, or in the glory reflected upon it by distinguished graduates, to the high standard worthy of the land of the Cavaliers, that was originally a wealthier and older colony than New England. Twenty thousand pounds might have lighted more brilliantly the torch of learning in the South, had the Utilitarian Walpole the imagination and greatness of soul enough, to take advantage of the opportunity which the voluntary presence of one of the greatest Europeans who ever trod the American continent offered him. Instead of doing so, Walpole sent in 1731, through the Bishop of London, this hypocritical answer to Berkeley's pleadings:

"If you put the question to me as a Minister, I must and can assure you that the money shall most undoubtedly be *paid, as soon as suits with public convenience*; but if you ask me as friend, whether Dean Berkeley should continue in America expecting the payment of £20,000, I advise him by all means to return home to Europe and to give up his present expectation."

If this is a fair specimen of the cynical treatment of

her Colonies by England, no wonder that forty-five years after, she lost her American possessions.

A few months after receiving this final answer, Berkeley, with his wife and infant son Henry, bade farewell to Rhode Island. They sailed from Boston in the fall of 1731, and on the following February found themselves back in London.

A brief sketch of Berkeley's activities during his stay, in his beloved Rhode Island, may be of interest. On his landing at Newport on a winter day early in 1729, he was cordially received by the inhabitants. The New England Weekly Courier of the time gives the following account of his arrival.

> "Yesterday arrived here Dean Berkeley of Londonderry, in a pretty large ship. He is a gentleman of middle stature, of an agreeable, pleasant, and erect aspect. He was ushered into the town with a great number of gentlemen, to whom he behaved himself after a very complaisant manner. 'Tis said he proposes to tarry here with his family about three months."

In the summer of 1729 he moved out of town to a quiet valley in the interior of the island, where he bought a farm, upon which he erected a neat frame-built home, which to this day is called Whitehall. Whitehall house, which has fallen to decay, was restored as late as 1900, as nearly as possible to the state in which Berkeley left it. In this island-home, Berkeley, to distract his mind from the anxieties imposed upon him by Walpole, resumed his studies. He would continue his meditations for hours either walking beneath the trees of his farm, or seated in a natural cave on the Newport shore, called "The Philosopher's Alcove," surmounted by overhanging rocks, and commanding an extensive view of the beach and ocean. In this secluded spot Berkeley, the buoyancy and versatility of whose genius neither anxiety nor loneliness could suppress, wrote the seven dialogues, which are now known to history as "Alciphron, or the Minute Philosopher." The purpose of this work as set forth by himself is, "to consider the Free-thinker in the various lights of atheist, libertine, enthusiast, scorner, critic, metaphysician, fatalist and sceptic." Alciphron, or the strong-minded man, represents sarcastically the daring atheist; Lysicles, the man of pleasure; while the keen-minded Euphranor, representing Berkeley, champions the cause of morality and religion. Crito is a friend of Euphranor. Berkeley calls the Free-thinkers "Minute Philosophers," because professing broad-mindedness, they really took a very narrow or minute view of life.

The work itself professes to be a refutation of the moral writings of Mandeville and Shaftesbury, and the atheism of Collins, all contemporaries of Berkeley. These dialogues ought to be attractive to every American, not only because "they are more fitted" as Fraser says, "than anything in English literature to recall the charm of Plato and Cicero," but also because they stand out as the first piece of refined and finished English literature written on American soil. Because of the several passages descriptive of the scenery of Berkeley's quiet retreat introduced into these dialogues, the associations of their literary charm will forever haunt the neighborhood of Newport. For instance here is a description of a scene near Whitehall, Berkeley's sea-girt home.

"Next morning Euphranor rose early, and spent the forenoon in ordering his affairs. After dinner we took our walk to Crito's which lay through half a dozen fields, planted round with plane trees, that are very common in this part of the country. We walked under the delicious shade of these trees for about an hour before we came to Crito's house, which stands in the middle of a small park, beautiful with two fine groves of oak and walnut and a winding stream of sweet clear water. We met a servant at the door with a small basket of fruit which he was carrying into a grove, where, he said, his master was with the two strangers. We found them all three sitting under a shade. And after the usual form of

first meeting, Euphranor and I sat down by them."
(First Dial. p. 24, Fraser.)

The activity of Berkeley in Newport—where for the
first time in his life he possessed what he could call a
home—was not confined to the writing of his dialogues.
Many threads of evidence testify to the extraordinary
social charm. His home at Whitehall was visited by the
Protestant missionaries of the time, from all parts of the
country. On Sundays, Quakers and Moravians, Jews and
Congregationalists, sixth-principle and seventh-principle
Baptists, and members of many other sects, which flour-
ished in the tolerant air of Roger Williams' Island retreat,
crowded the Episcopal Church, standing even in the aisles,
to listen to the edifying discourses of the learned philan-
thropist. Berkeley founded at Newport a Philosophical
Society, which has left as a legacy to the present day, a
valuable public library to that summer retreat.

IV

Berkeley, during his stay in Rhode Island, was not
indifferent to the spread of his philosophical Immaterial-
ism. He made one distinguished convert to his system—
Dr. Samuel Johnson, of Stratford, Conn. (1696-1772).
Johnson, who became an able expositor of Berkeleyanism,
was the earliest of our native Idealists. As a boy he
attended Saybrook School, Conn., which in after years,
became the present Yale College. Whilst tutor in Saybrook or Yale, Johnson abandoned Puritanism and became
an Anglican. He visited England and there was ordained
a minister of the Angelican church. Learning at this
time in the Colonies was at its lowest ebb. The learned
Puritans of the first generations having died out, their
successors were mere pedants. Chandler, the earliest
biographer of Johnson, tells us that "What the Metaphysics taught at Yale at this time was not fit for worms."
While Johnson was a teacher at Yale, another great original thinker of the time, the mystic Jonathan Edwards
of Northampton fame, was his pupil. Edwards subsequently, in order to defend the atrocious doctrine of

Puritanism, the utter depravity of human nature, wrote the ablest treatise in the English language against the freedom of the will. Edwards was expelled by his congregation from Northampton, yet despite his misfortunes and fantastic doctrines, the unselfishness and nobility of soul which he manifested by consecrating his life to the welfare of the Indian tribes at Stockbridge in the Berkshires, still challenge our admiration.

Would it not have been reasonable to expect that these three men, the accomplished Berkeley, the enthusiastic Johnson and the mystical-minded Jonathan Edwards, then contemporaries in New England, would by their influence have lighted the spark of original thought in colonial America, that would in due time develop into a native born American philosophy? Johnson's subsequent career placed him in a position of wide influence over the young men of his day. He was the first choice as head of the Philadelphia Academy, now the University of Pennsylvania. He was the first president of King's College, New York, now Columbia University. Harvard was already in existence and Princeton had begun its career. Johnson, too, had written the 'Elements of Philosophy' from the Berkeleyan standpoint, which was used as a text-book in classes of his own New York College, and through the influence of Franklin, who defrayed the expenses of publishing the book, was also introduced into the Philadelphia Academy. Yet the influence and efforts of these men fell still-born on the land. And to this day, America has no native school of thought, if we except, perhaps the remnants of neglected trifles stuffed into the system of Mrs. Eddy. Many reasons may be suggested to explain this apathy towards philosophy.

In New York the spirit of commercialism then choked off, just as it is doing today, any abiding taste for meditative thought. Philadelphia was then immersed in the tide of Materialism that flowed in upon it from England. Harvard was so wrapped up in its armor of Puritanism that it was impervious to the prick of a foreign lance however keen. Princeton was dominated by the common-sense philosophy of the Scotchman Reid that execrated the Idealism of Berkeley. The Revolution that burst upon America towards the end of the century was then brewing, and the fact that Johnson was an Episcopalian minister militated against his influence among the dissenting sects in colony-days who had no love for the established Church of England. The fundamental reason perhaps why America yesterday or today has not yet developed the "Philosophic brow that comes with years" is because a young country naturally engages all its energies, not in the development of its spiritual resources of thought, but in the immediate needs of its material advancement. Berkeley, in the character of Euphranor well expresses it, saying:

"I have long observed that there is a gradual progress in human affairs. The first care of mankind is to supply the cravings of nature; in the second place they study the conveniences and comforts of life. But the subduing prejudices, and acquiring true knowledge, that Herculean labor, is the last, being what demands the most perfect abilities, and to which all other advantages are preparative. Right, said Euphranor, Alciphron hath touched our true defect. It was always my opinion that as soon as we had provided subsistence for the body our next care should be to improve our minds. But the desire of wealth steps between, and engrosseth man's thoughts." (Alcip. First D. p. 30-35.)

Berkeley's three companions, James, Dalton, and Smibert, settled in Boston. They endeavored, but failed to lure Berkeley from Newport to the city of the Puritans. He preferred the quiet of his country home, and never traveled about in the colonies. He loved Rhode Island and would have been glad to plant his college there, rather than in the Bermudas. Mr. Smibert was the artist of the party and his paintings yet adorn many Rhode Island homes. Mr. James, afterwards Sir John James, the most prominent of Berkeley's companions, became a convert to the Catholic Church.

Berkeley, before leaving Rhode Island, gave lasting proofs of his generosity and interest in American education. His Rhode Island farm he donated to Yale, to found a graduate school in that college. The proceeds of this property was to be used to maintain three scholars during the time between their first and second degrees. No doubt he was the first benefactor in America to endow a graduate school. Over two hundred scholars enjoyed the fruits of this benefaction, among them two college presidents—President Wheelock, the founder, more than a century ago, of Dartmouth College, and Timothy Dwight, president of Yale College (1795-1817.) Dartmouth was originally founded for the education of the Indians. I wonder if Berkeley's interest in the Indians had anything to do with determining the purpose of their project? To Yale, Berkeley also donated nearly one thousand select volumes, and made a similar gift to Harvard. An oil painting of Berkeley, the work of Smibert, has still an honored place in Yale. The Yale Berkeley School of Divinity also perpetuates his name. At the extreme limit of the American continent, towards which "the course of empire takes its way," the present seat of the University of California, at the suggestion of a late President of Johns Hopkins, is appropriately named Berkeley. Trinity Church, Newport, still contains Berkeley's organ. "His offer of an organ to a church in the town of Berkeley, Mass.," Fraser tells us, "is said to have been too much for the Puritanical rigor of the inhabitants, who unanimously voted it an invention of the devil to entrap the souls of men." Despite this ancient intractableness of New England, which must have amused Berkeley, there will still exist academic shrines to his memory as long as this country shall endure.

In our day, historians have searched the documentary annals of our country, to discover and reveal the contributions of Ireland to the greatness of America. May we not justly claim, that the facts here set forth give Ireland, in the person of Berkeley, an honored place as a contributor to the intellectual development of the United

States? May we not reasonably surmise that his broader intellectual vision helped to strengthen the desire of liberty in colonial America, which was, about forty-five years later, demanded of England at the point of the sword?

V

Berkeley on his return to Ireland had yet about twenty years to live. He was appointed Bishop of Cloyne, County Cork, in 1734. This period of his life, with all its old enthusiasm, was devoted to the benevolent service of his country. His thoughts at this time took on a turn for sociological rather than for purely philosophical writings. He became intensely interested in the economical improvement of his country. Ireland had then its own parliament, entirely Protestant though it was. It was one of Berkeley's highest boasts, as Sir James Mackintosh remarks, "that, though his father was of English extraction, he was a true Irishman, and the first eminent Protestant, who avowed his love for all his countrymen." For this reason his Catholic fellow-countrymen bore public testimony to his liberality and worth. The one blot on Berkeley's character is, that he never raised his voice or pen in protesting against the Penal Laws.

In 1735, he published the "Querist," a book which contains a series of brief questions without answers, "presented" as Fraser says, "with an originality of literary art, combined with humor and irony, which makes the work more interesting than any similar book in English literature." It pictures two Irelands—Protestant Ireland, whose only outlook on life was, not to advance the industrial development of their country, but as is the wont of the rich and dominant classes of every country in the world, in sporting, fox-hunting, gambling and riotous living, to squander the estates they acquired by confiscation; and Catholic Ireland, the abject condition of which he suggests, by the following questions: "Whether there be upon earth, any Christian or civilized people, so beggarly, wretched, and destitute as the common Irish?" (N. 132) Other specimens of these questions are:

No. 39. Whether in the wastes of America a man might not possess twenty miles square of land, and yet want his dinner, or a coat to his back?

141. Whether a woman of fashion ought not to be declared a public enemy?

199. Whether it was not an Irish professor, who first opened the public schools of Oxford? Whether this island had not been anciently famous for learning?

201. Whether the gentleman of estate had a right to be idle; and whether he ought not to be the great promoter and director of industry among his tenants and neighbors?

Whether it was not a vain attempt (by England) to project the flourishing of our Protestant gentry, exclusive of the bulk of the natives?

His last question, number 595, is pathetic, if not reminiscent of one of the unrighted wrongs of history:

Whose fault is it, if poor Ireland still continues poor?

Berkeley from 1734 to 1752, as the Episcopal Bishop of Cloyne, devoted himself to missionary work and the relief of the poor among his people. Fevers and "flu" seem to have prevailed in his diocese. As a remedy for these diseases and indeed as a panacea, he administered Tar-water, a medicine he learned from the American Indians. In his declining years he published "Siris," a work on the virtue of tar-water interspersed with Platonic speculations on a variety of subjects. In 1752 he went to Oxford to live, and there in 1753, he died.

Thus ended the remarkable career of a man, who, in the words of Prof. Alexander, "was a man of extraordinary intellectual ability, and of exquisite purity and generosity of character." (Hist. of Phil., p. 223.)

CHAPTER VII

PHILOSOPHICAL SYSTEM

George Berkeley (1685-1753)

WE make no apology for the rather lengthy biography of Berkeley. His three years' residence in Newport, Rhode Island, during which he exerted considerable influence over the early philosophical schools of Colonial America, and his sanguine, though perhaps visionary hopes of establishing in the new world a civilization superior to that of the bigoted, persecuting, materialistic state of society that so disgusted him in the English world of the eighteenth century, by means of his projected Bermuda College, justify our more than usual interest in the career of this distinguished Irishman. Moreover, the fairy-like character of his spiritualistic philosophy may be better appreciated when viewed as the expression and counterpart of a life so romantic, unselfish and other-worldly as was his.

What then was this unique philosophy which this extraordinary man hoped would be decisive in counteracting the materialism and sceptical free-thinking of his time? We find that every modern philosopher, like a daring knight-errant, sets out with the noble purpose of reforming the prevailing system of his time, and of restoring to humanity uncontrovertible truth and certainty, with the result, that his new system is again engulfed in the very scepticism which he would avoid. In Berkeley's youth, Locke was the dominant philosopher of the English non-Catholic world. So interested was Berkeley in Locke's "Essay Concerning the Human Understanding," that he organized, during his undergraduate days in Trinity College, Dublin, a society for the express purpose of studying Locke's "new philosophy." Berkeley, however, was not a meek follower of his master Locke. His aim was not merely to absorb Locke's teaching and rest satisfied. His attitude toward Locke was critical and reformative. With a keener and more logical mind than Locke, he successfully exposed the latter's inconsistencies and contradictions, and logically deduced from Locke's fundamental principles his own peculiar, idealistic system. Berkeley, is, in fact, Locke made more consistent and logical.

It will not be difficult, then, to understand the system of Berkeley, if, at the start, we grasp the fundamental principle of all Idealism, which Berkeley took over from Locke, as Locke adopted it from Descartes—a principal which very many leaders of modern thought even to the present day, have accepted as axiomatic. This principle we cannot too often repeat. It was thus expressed by Locke . . . "the word *Idea* serves best for whatsoever is the *object* of the understanding when a man thinks" (Introd. 8.) Again Locke says, "Since the mind of man, in all its thoughts and reasonings, hath no other object but its own ideas, it is evident that our knowledge is only conversant about them" (B. IV. C. I. 1.) Again Locke states: "Knowledge then seems to me to be nothing but the perception of the connection and agreement, or disagreement, and repugnancy of any of our ideas" (B. II. C. I. 2.) The principle variously expressed in the above quotations from Locke may be thus briefly stated—"The direct, and, immediate objects which the human mind knows, whether by sense or intellect, are not any really existing objects outside and independent of the knowing mind, but objects lying wholly within the mind, psychical facts, that are variously termed ideas, impressions, phenomena, sensations, feelings, states of consciousness." Professor Case has admirably and tersely expressed, and indicated the historical importance of this same principle thus—"Psychological Idealism began with the supposition of Descartes that all the immediate objects of knowledge are ideas. From Descartes it passed to Locke and Berkeley. But with Hume it changed its terms from ideas to impressions. Kant preferred phenomena, Mill sensations. The most usual terms of the present day are sensations, feelings, psychical phenomena and states of consciousness" ("Physical Realism" p. 15.)

Now, we may recall, that, though all those leaders of modern thought adopted the idealistic principle, yet some of them, starting from the psychical facts, professed to demonstrate the existence of realities outside and beyond those facts. In other words, they endeavor to infer what actually exists from what is merely ideal. For example, Descartes, as you may readily recall, starting from the mere idea of God—a psychical object of knowledge—attempted to prove both the real existence of God and the existence of the physical world. Locke also endeavored to prove "through the intervention of ideas," the actual existence of bodies outside of him. Whereas the key to Berkeley's position and philosophical system may be easily grasped, if we bear in mind that he persistently maintained, with all the subtlety of his genius and masterly style, that *psychical facts,* which in common with Descartes and Locke he held to be the direct and immediate objects of knowledge, could never yield by any process of logical demonstration or inference the *physical existence* of matter outside of him. In other words *psychical premises,* call them ideas or whatever you will, can never produce a *physical conclusion,* for the simple reason that the conclusion cannot contain more than is contained in the premises. We are inclined to think that Berkeley's contention is logically unassailable. If the mind is confined in its direct perceptions to its own subjective states and is cut off from the direct and immediate knowledge of the outside world, then, Berkeley argues, how is it to know whether its subjective ideas do, or do not conform to or represent extramental realities. Locke maintained that his ideas represented outside objects, and directly knowing his ideas he professed to know what they represented. But, says Berkeley, in order to know that ideas represent actually existing objects outside and independent of themselves, it would be necessary to compare the ideas with the extramental objects. But we cannot compare our ideas with the objects they are supposed to represent, because as Locke admitted, we know only the ideas. Comparison demands the knowledge of both the ideas and the realities in order to discover whether the ideas represent the realities. Hence we can never escape, Berkeley insists, from the net of our own ideas, and consequently we can never know that material bodies exist outside of us. Not only did Berkeley point out to Locke and to his admirers who adopted his idealistic principle, that they could never know that matter exists outside of them, but by a puzzling net of sophistry woven by his Celtic subtlety, that it was a contradiction to say that anyone could perceive an unperceived object like external matter. If you perceive matter, then it is an "idea" according to Locke and not an independently existing unperceived something. Nobody believed Berkeley but few could answer him.

Thus did Berkeley expose the fallacy of Locke's "Representative Realism." And ignoring of course, the "Presentational Realism of Scholasticism," Berkeley with a few strokes of his pen, triumphantly annihilated the external world. Once the existence of matter, as an independent reality outside the mind, was swept away, the whole tribe of Materialists like Hobbes and Materialistic Pantheists like Toland, were not left a shred of a foundation for the erection of their Atheistical and Materialistic structures. The refutation of those schools of thought was the inspiring purpose that stimulated and directed the course of Berkeley's future thought. We do not know exactly when this far-reaching conclusion from Locke's principle flashed across his mind. It must have been very early in life, because his conviction of its justness touched the point of enthusiasm, when he recorded in his "Common Place Book," (a kind of diary, wherein he jotted down his stray thoughts during his student days,) the following record—"I wonder not at my sagacity in discovering this obvious and amazing truth. I rather wonder at my stupid inadvertence in not finding it out before." Berkeley was a keener logician than Locke.

The kernel of Berkeley's whole position may be gleaned

from the following passages from his "Principles of Human Knowledge," published in 1710, when he was only twenty-four years of age. Berkeley evidently asked himself, as Kant did, "what can I know?" and for answer set forth the following classes of objects which the human mind is capable of knowing. Thus:

1. "It is evident to any one who takes a survey of the objects of human knowledge, that they are either ideas actually imprinted on the senses; or else such as are perceived by attending to the passions and operations of the mind; or lastly *ideas* formed by help of memory and imagination—either compounding, dividing, or barely representing those originally perceived in the aforesaid ways. By sight I have the ideas of light and colors, with their several degrees and variations. By touch I perceive hard and soft, heat and cold, motion and resistance, and among these more or less either as to quantity or degrees. Smelling furnishes me with odors; the palate with tastes, and hearing conveys sounds to the mind in all their variety of tone and composition." Pr. 1. Berkeley falls into the same errors as Locke in asserting that the sense can perceive an *abstraction*, color, etc., and not something qualified by color—a colored thing. Remark also that he follows Locke in attributing to the term "idea" a sensistic meaning.

"And as several of these are observed to accompany each other, they come to be marked by one name, and so be reputed as one *thing*. Thus, for example, a certain color, taste, smell, figure and consistence have been observed to go together, are accounted one distinct thing, signified by the name apple; other *collections of ideas* constitute a stone, a tree, a book, and the like sensible things; which as they are pleasing or disagreeable excite the passions of love, hatred, joy, grief and so forth." (Pr. 1.) Locke also maintained that things like apple, stone or tree were only a collection or cluster of "qualities," except that Locke *professed* that the "primary qualities" of bodies existed outside the mind, whereas Berkeley maintained that they existed only within the mind. Indeed, Berkeley's denial of the existence outside the mind of both material qualities and material sub-stances was made plausible as a logical conclusion of Locke's declaration that substance was nothing more than "a *supposed, imagined, unknown* support of qualities—a mere creation of the mind."

2. "But besides all that endless variety of ideas or objects of knowledge, there is likewise something that knows or perceives them and exercises divers operations, as willing, imagining, remembering, about them. This perceiving, acting being is what I call *mind, spirit, soul* or *myself.* By which words I do not denote any one of my ideas, but a thing entirely distinct from them *wherein they exist* or which is the same thing, whereby they are perceived; for the existence of an idea consists in being perceived." (Pr. 2.). Thus did Berkeley admit the existence of spiritual substance, while he denied outright the existence of any material substance.

3. "That neither our thoughts, nor passions, nor ideas formed by the imagination, exist without the mind, is what everybody will allow, and to me it seems no less evident that the various sensations or ideas imprinted on the Sense, however blended or combined together (that is, whatever objects they compose,) cannot exist otherwise than in a mind perceiving them. I think an intuitive knowledge may be obtained of this, that is, that matter depends for its real existence on a percipient mind, by anyone that shall attend to what is meant by the term *exist* when applied to sensible things. The table I wrote on I say exists; that is *I see and feel it,* and if I were out of my study, I should say it existed—meaning thereby, that if I were in my study, I might perceive it, or that some other spirit actually does perceive it. There was an odor, that is, *it was smelt,* there was a sound, that is *it was heard*; a color or figure and *it was perceived by sight or touch.* This is all I can understand by these and like expressions. Extinguish spirit, then, and what we call the material would cease to exist. For as to what is said of the *absolute* existence of unthinking things, without any rela-

tion to their being perceived, that is to me perfectly un-
intelligible. Their *"esse est percipi;"* nor is it possible
they should have any existence out of the minds of thinking things which perceive them." (Prin. 3.) "Existence," then, for Berkeley means "to be perceived" by a
mind or spirit. What is not perceived does not exist.

Thus does the keen mind of Berkeley expose for all
time the blundering illogicality of Descartes, and John
Locke, in adopting the root principle of Idealism and in
professing at the same time to be Realists.

Berkeley, having made the material universe disappear
by one flourish of his magic wand of logic, what realities,
we may ask, did his Idealism, so far, leave in existence?
A review of the first three "Principles of Knowledge,"
which we have quoted, will reveal to us those objects.

1.   First in order are: *"ideas actually imprinted on
the senses."* Those ideas of course are sensuous. They
are the direct and immediate objects of our perceptions.
They are mind-dependent. They are neither the representations, or the *means*, of knowing any objects beyond
and independent of themselves. What ordinary people
call an apple or an orange or a table, is, for Berkeley,
merely an *idea-object*, or a cluster of ideas, which accompany one another and make up an idea-thing. *The ideas
are themselves the things.* We do not evolve these idea-
objects from our inner consciousness, because with regard to them, we are conscious of being *passive* not *active*.
They are not innate. They are "imprinted on the senses"
by some cause extrinsic to ourselves. What this cause is,
we shall learn later.

2.   There is another set of objects which we know,
namely, "the passions and operations of the mind." Those
objects are not ideas. They are not "imprinted on our
senses by any outward cause." The passions of love,
hatred, joy, grief and so forth, are excited naturally in
us, according as the clusters of ideas which are the idea-
things, such as a book, a landscape, a flower and so forth,
are pleasing or displeasing to us. "The operations" of the
mind spring, of course, from the mind as an active cause.

3. Lastly, "there is likewise something which knows and perceives all that endless variety of ideas and passions and operations previously enumerated. This *something* not only *perceives* but also exercises divers operations as willing, imagining, remembering. This perceiving, acting being is our *soul, mind, spirit, myself*." (Prin. 2.) (a) *Ideas,* or idea-objects which ordinary people recognize as external objects, as mountains, lakes, rivers, etc., Berkeley asserts have no existence outside the mind that perceives them; their *"esse est percipi;"* their existence consists in their being perceived. All those things which we call the outside world are only an unsubstantial vision, idea-objects, that have no existence outside some perceiving mind. Berkeley's denial of the existence of extra-mental objects may have been suggested by Locke. Locke admitted that he was not *certain* of the existence of objects outside his own mind. For he declared that the external existence of material objects did not rise to the dignity of "knowledge." The external existence of material objects, according to Locke, falls short of "knowledge." In Locke's phraseology, "knowledge" is identical with certainty." Instead of acknowledging that he had "knowledge" or "certainty" of things outside of him, he declares that he had only "assurance" not "knowledge" of such objects. And "assurance" for Locke, means only "blind faith" or Reid's "blind instinct." Berkeley rejected the flimsy guarantee of "assurance" or "blind faith or instinct" and denied outright that material objects exist outside a mind. For Berkeley the complete definition of "existence" consists either in *"percipi"* (being perceived) or *"percipere"* (perceiving). Hence when that which ordinary folk call an external object *is not perceived* by some mind, it ceases to exist. In like manner a mind or soul or spirit if it should cease *to perceive,* that mind, soul or spirit would cease to exist. Even in sleep the spirit or soul must, therefore, according to Berkeley, be actually *perceiving.* The essence of soul or spirit is, therefore, *to perceive,* as the essence of the existence of material objects consists in *being perceived.* The similarity between Berkeley's and

Descartes' views on the essence of soul or spirit is obvious. For Descartes *thought* is the essence of soul, for Berkeley, unceasing *perception*.

(b) *Passions*, operations, phantasms have likewise, as everybody admits, no existence outside of the perceiving mind or spirit.

(c) *Lastly*, there is the perceiving something, myself, soul or spirit. By self, soul or spirit Berkeley means not one of his "ideas," but a thing entirely distinct from them, wherein they exist. The *"esse"* or being or essence of "ideas" consists in their *"percipi,"* whereas the *"esse"* or essence or "spirit" consists in *"percipere."* No "idea" of "spirit" can be formed. An "idea" is passive, inert, "spirit" is active. An "idea" is a sensuous image. No sensuous image can be formed of "spirit." But Berkeley teaches, that, though we cannot form an "idea" in the Berkeleyan sense of "spirit", we can have a "notion" of spirit. It has some meaning for us. Berkeley thus distinguishes an "idea" from a "notion," (Pr. 27,) though in several passages in his "Principles" he uses "notion" and "idea" as synonymous. On Berkeley's argument in defense of our knowledge of a substantial *spirit,* because we can have a *notion* of it, and his rejection of a *material* external *substance,* because we can have only an *idea* of it, Ueberweg's Commentary is enlightening.

Ueberweg says, "whether our consciousness of the psychical should be designated by the term "idea" or 'notion' is rather a question of verbal than of practical interest. It is worthy of remark, however, that if we propose to designate the 'notions' of the mind in regard to other minds and their operations, as *objects* of cognition, in the manner in which Berkeley in the case of sense-perception designates "ideas" as the *objects* perceived, using in part the same arguments on which he has grounded the conclusion that we know only our own ideas, and not bodies which are external to our mind, it would warrant the inference that we know only our own 'notions' of spirits and not spirits themselves, which have an existence outside of our own.   Berkeley's arguments would lead to the acceptance of the sole existence of the person arguing,—to what is called 'theoretic egoism' or 'solipsism'."   Krauth, p. 355-6.

(d) We have other "ideas" of which the will is the source through the exercise of the imagination. But because the "ideas" imprinted on our minds from without and which are the real things, that is idea-things, are more lively and forcible, less dependent on the percipient spirit, than are the "ideas" of mere imagination, hence Berkeley distinguishes the "ideas" of sense from the "ideas" of imagination. Hume later on calls the "ideas" imprinted on the sense, "impressions" and reserves the term "idea" for the weaker and paler "ideas" of the imagination.

All the objects of knowledge which Berkeley enumerates as existing and capable of being known by us, are not yet completed. He acknowledges that other (1) human spirits, like our own, and (2) God also exist, and that both can be known by us.

He endeavors to establish the existence of other human spirits by the following argument. We are intuitively aware of our own existence. "We comprehend our own existence by inward *feeling*. In two ways we know ourself. (1) I am immediately aware of the existence of my ideas as *mine*. I know that I do not cause them, because I am *passive* in their regard. They are imprinted on my senses, but I know that it is I who perceives them. (2) I have also an immediate feeling or sense-consciousness of *activity*. In the first place (a) I know that I cause mental images, and I likewise exercise (b) both productive and constructive imagination in the formation of my mental images, and (c) I know my acts of volition in the construction of these images. My own conscious experience then, assures me of the existence of myself immediately. (In this argument you may notice that Berkeley implicitly admits the principle of *causality*, but that the only existing cause is *spirit*.) The existence of other human spirits is not immediately known to me. I know them only by *inference*. This inference is based upon the activity of finite spirits in exciting ideas in me."

Berkeley argues thus: "I perceive several motions, changes and combinations of ideas, that inform me there are certain particular agents, like myself, which accompany them, and concur in their production. Hence the knowledge I have of other spirits is not immediate as is the knowledge of my ideas; but depending on the invention of ideas, by me referred to agents distinct from myself, as effects or concomitant signs." (Prin. 145.) Dr. Johnston, in his recent book (1923) "The Development of Berkeley's Philosophy," elucidates this argument by expressing it in simple fashion. He writes "I make a box. When I look at it, a certain presentation, that is an 'idea' of a box is before or in my mind. This presentation is ultimately caused by God, but the box which I make is in some way the *occasion* of it. Now if a presentation, similar to the one which I have, when I look at the box that I have made, is excited in my mind, at another time and place, I infer that its occasion is a box similar to the one made by me. Now, as I did not make the box myself, I infer that it was made by some other finite spirit, like myself. Other finite spirits therefore exist." (p. 195.) The weakness and inconsistency of this argument is discussed by Ueberweg. (Note 114-Krauth).

Furthermore Berkeley admitted that God was an object of our knowledge. His argument is stated in Pr. 26. He says: "We conceive a continual succession of ideas; some are anew excited, others are totally changed or totally disappear. There is, therefore, some cause of those ideas, whereon they depend (i.e. for their existence,) and which produces and changes them. That this cause cannot be any quality or idea or combination of *ideas* is clear from the preceding sections." (In this section Berkeley says that ideas are wholly passive and inert; it is impossible for an idea, to do anything, as it is impossible for a quality to exist of itself.) "It, (the cause of my ideas) must therefore be a *substance*; but it has been shown that there

is no corporeal or material substance: it remains, therefore, that the cause of ideas is an incorporeal active substance or spirit." And this spirit that causes or imprints
ideas in the mind is God. Locke may have suggested to
Berkeley that God was the direct cause of his "ideas,"
because Locke said, "I see or perceive or I have ideas
when it pleases God that I should, but in a way I cannot
comprehend." Johnson, p. 51.

Now Berkeley asks the significant question, where are
the idea-objects during the intervals of my non-perception
of them? Suppose I hold in my hand an orange and perceive the idea-orange, and then drop it and turn away my
eyes. The orange, that is the idea-orange is no longer
perceived by me. It has not for me any "percipi." Does
the orange (idea-orange) then cease to exist? Is it annihilated? No, replies Berkeley, it may exist, as an *idea*
in some other finite spirit. Because if it exists at all, it
must exist in some spirit. But suppose all finite spirits
ceased to exist, would matter then, to wit, the idea-matter
also cease to exist? Again Berkeley answers, then the
idea-matter would exist in the Infinite Spirit of God. For
Berkeley therefore, the natural or real existence of the
material world, that is the idea-material world, is impossible, meaningless, in the absence of some spirit, finite or
infinite that perceives it. "For," he says, "it is plainly
repugnant that any one of these (i.e. idea-things) or combination of them, should exist *unperceived*" (Pr. 4.)

This extraordinary system of Berkeley is known in the
History of Thought by many different names which suggest the gist of the theory. It is called "Acosmothetic
Idealism," because it denies the separate and independent
existence of the Cosmos or material world. It is designated
"Spiritualistic Pluralism," because it admits the substantial existence of many finite spirits and of the Infinite
Spirit, God. Some term it "Objective Idealism" because it
admits as objects of knowledge real substances, namely
spirits, while it is Idealism only, in so far as it denies the
existence of substantial matter in the world. It is thus
differentiated from the Phenomenal Idealism of Hume and

of William James, which admits only an ever flowing series of a cluster of perceptions without any substantial spirit to sustain them,—"the stream of consciousness" of William James. Berkeley's Idealism is different also from the thorough-going or subjective Idealism of Fichte, which admits only one Pantheistic Spirit evolving all things, that is, all ideas, from its own inner activity.

Strange as it may appear to the ordinary man, it is certainly true, that Idealism in one form or another has captured the great majority of modern non-Catholic thinkers. "In its *principle of cognition*" says Krauth, "Idealism is so strong as to have carried nearly the entire body of thinkers with it—generic Idealism is the predominant system of the world." (Berkeley's Principles p. 66.) Of course the "world" of Idealists studiously ignored the great body of Catholic thinkers. But we must not lose sight of the fact that Idealists form only a very insignificant minority, when we compare them with the vast majority of common-sense people in the world. The Idealists have written cart-loads of books in defense of their system, the burden of proof lies with them, yet they have failed to convince the world of the truth of their theory. Berkeley in his eagerness to destroy Materialism fell into the contrary extreme of Spiritualistic Idealism. No violent extremes endure. A sober moderation stands secure.

Like all extreme and exaggerated systems, Idealism has stumbled upon a great and deep truth. It is this. Matter does ultimately both for its existence and intelligibility depend upon the mind or spirit and not spirit upon matter. Because God, who is spirit created matter. Matter then depends for its existence and conservation, on the Infinite Spirit, rather than spirit upon matter. This is the truth which the human mind instinctively clings to. This does not mean however that the various material objects in the universe are mere ideas of God, or ideas imprinted by God upon finite spirits. Material objects have their own existence outside and distinct from the ideas of them.

CHAPTER VIII

A CRITICISM OF BERKELEYISM

WITH a precocity unparalleled by any modern philosopher, Berkeley wrote his "Principles of Knowledge" at the early age of twenty-four. In this treatise of one hundred and fifty-six sections, remarkable for its subtlety of thought and charm of style, he embodied the answer to the question—"What are the objects of human knowledge?" These objects which Berkeley professed to know were set forth in our previous chapter.

To the ordinary man the shock of surprise comes, not from an enumeration of the objects whose existence Berkeley admits, namely; (1) ideas, (2) his own mind or spirit or self, (3) other spirits, and (4) God, but rather from what he persistently denies, namely the independent existence of external bodies, or the whole material universe, which of course, involves the denial of the real existence of one's own body. It is this denial that aroused the ridicule of Berkeley's contemporary critics. Byron wrote for instance:—

"When Bishop Berkeley said 'There was no matter,'
   And proved it; 'twas no matter what he said,
   They say his system 'tis in vain to batter,
   Too subtle for the airiest human head,
   And yet who can believe it?"

And Dr. Samuel Johnson, when a gentleman who was defending Berkeley's views was about going away, said:— Pray, Sir, don't leave us, for we may perhaps forget to think of you, and you will cease to exist. (Krauth, pp. 42-46.)

This facetious remark of Dr. Johnson, Berkeley attempts to answer. He says:—"For though we hold, indeed the objects of sense to be nothing else but "ideas" which cannot exist unperceived, yet we may not hence conclude, that they have no existence except only while they are perceived by *us*, since there may be some other spirit that perceives them though we do not." (Principle 48.) The answer of Berkeley is not satisfactory, because it must be supposed that there is only one gentleman in the case. But the gentleman that Johnson saw was not numerically the same gentleman whom the other spirit perceived. In fact there were as many distinct gentlemen in the case as there were percipient spirits. Each spirit perceived its own idea-gentleman which was not the same idea-gentleman as was perceived by each of the other spirits. And yet it must be assumed that there was only one gentleman in the case.

"Add to this," says Ueberweg, "that there are frequently intervals during which no one (no created spirit) perceived particular objects. Are we, for instance to say that the Herculanean Manuscripts did not exist during the centuries through which they remained buried, and that God at a later period created them anew? The restoration certainly is not to be explained by an order established by natural laws. This order subsists only in case that there is an existence without all (finite) minds during the interval. The existence in the divine mind cannot explain the permanence of the object, inasmuch as this supposition would *involve too much*, to wit, an eternal existence of the object, which nevertheless has a beginning and an end in time; there must, consequently, be an object distinct from God's idea of the object, which subsists during the interval in which no finite spirit perceives it." (Krauth, pp. 366-7.)

The classical argument, which the philosophical critics of Berkeley commonly make use of, is based upon the *veracity, wisdom,* and *goodness* of God, whose existence Berkeley admits. Our pious author teaches that it is not material objects outside of us that excite in us certain sensations, because no such material objects exist, but that it is God that directly causes our subjective sensations, which he calls "ideas." The inevitable result is that we now have an unconquerable, incorrigible conviction that bodies exist outside of us, and have no means of correcting the illusion. God would then deliberately lead us into positive invincible error. But such action on God's part would be at variance with, nay contradictory of, His infinite veracity, goodness and wisdom. But Berkeley would reply—"Accept my doctrine that you perceive those God-given "ideas" only; and abide by its consequences, and then you will correct the illusion and get rid of the deception of the existence of the material world."

To which the ordinary man may answer—"It is absolutely impossible for me to rid myself of the primitive and intuitional report of my senses that bodies exist outside and independently of me. I am powerless to reconstruct a world in which nothing more exists but "spirits" and their "ideas." To do so would mean that I divest myself of my nature and adopt another. We may by an effort imagine for a short time that bodies are phantoms, but do what we will we cannot sustain for a length of time that imaginary attitude—no man can.

"Naturam expellas furca, tamen usque recurrit."

The little child in its nurse's arms will stretch out its tiny hand and point to the moon, and beseechingly cry to its nurse to give it the moon as a plaything. If under normal conditions our senses, and for that matter each of our cognitive faculties do not by their very nature reveal to us infallibly things as they are, then must we despair of ever knowing anything and universal scepticism is inevitable.

We may reasonably ask, why does Berkeley so confidently trust his intellect and its function reason which reveals to him the existence of his own spirit or self, when he says "there is likewise Something which knows or perceives them (ideas)—my soul, spirit, myself?"

Why does he not distrust his consciousness which tells him that he has "ideas?" Why respect the natural functioning of these cognitive faculties and pick out the senses as the butt of his distrust? Are not the humble senses God-given cognitive faculties in their own sphere? Are they not part of our human nature and given and intended by nature, that is, by God, for the definite purpose of knowing? Why distrust the deliverances of nature in the case of the senses and confide in nature's deliverances in the case of the other faculties?

But Berkeley may reply, I do not distrust the senses so long as they are employed in perceiving those objects for which they were intended by nature. For instance I say "by touch I perceive hard and soft, heat and cold, motion and resistance; smelling furnishes with odours; the palate with tastes; and hearing conveys sounds to the mind———. The table I write on I say exists; that is, I see and feel it———. There was an odour, that is, it was smelt; there was a sound, that is, it was heard; a colour or figure and it was perceived by sight or touch."

The ordinary man who understands Berkeley's system may quietly remark "Do you not admit, Mr. Berkeley, that in your system, 'light' and 'colors'; 'hard' and 'soft'; 'heat' and 'cold'; 'motion' and 'resistance'; 'odours' and 'tastes'; even 'the table that you write on' have no existence outside the mind, but are merely 'ideas' in the mind? So are what you term mountains, lakes, and trees etc., merely subjective 'ideas,' that is, psychical phenomena, intramental appearances or phantoms. Now, Mr. Berkeley it is not the external senses that perceive intra-mental, phenomenal 'ideas.' Such 'ideas' are objects of consciousness and imagination—of consciousness, because 'ideas' are intra-mental, psychical facts; of imagination because they are extended picturable phenomena before the mind. Consciousness and imagination are alone required to perceive all your 'ideas.' "

"Again to establish the existence of your own spirit or self and the existence of other spirits, that is, other people, and the existence of God, even if you did validly and logically establish all these existences, though one may well be sceptical of your success in so doing, intellect and its function of reason come into play. All the really existing objects, then, which you admit are, therefore, objects of either your own consciousness, imagination, namely your personal "ideas," or are the objects of intellect or reason, as are your own substantial spirit, other human spirits and God. What objects are then left for the external senses about which you are continually speaking in your writings? You must admit that there are no objects in your world of "spirits" and their "ideas" that demand the external senses. You ought, then, to omit the external senses altogether. In your system the external senses are not needed. They exist for no purpose. Why, then, admit their existence at all?"

Moreover, it seems to be beyond the pale of comprehension to understand how it is possible for "a spirit" to be endowed with sense faculties whether external or internal, such as the imagination for instance and sensuous memory. Whether Berkeley conceives these cognitive faculties as really distinct from the "spirit" or not, they must necessarily be spiritual. If the sense-faculties are not really distinct from, but are merely functions of the spirit, these functions cannot be otherwise than spiritual. If the sense-faculties are really distinct from the spirit, they are still rooted in the spirit alone, consequently must be spiritual. To speak, then, of, seeing, tasting, smelling, touching, hearing and imagining as spiritual acts is an abuse of language and an arbitrary changing of the ordinary signification of words.

Again, how is it possible that such extended "ideas" as Berkeley speaks of, as, idea-rivers etc., can be subjected in a pure spirit, such as he says he is. That extended ideas reside in an unextended spirit is as impossible to understand as that a pure spirit can be endowed with sense-faculties. To say that "spirit" has senses is as incomprehensible as to say that brute matter possesses intellect.

Again Berkeley seems to consider the distinction between "notion" and "idea" to be of vital importance. We have a "notion" he says but not an "idea" of spirit, though in Principles 5 and 25 he fails to make the distinction. In these Principles "notion" and "idea" are synonymous. We have, then, a "notion" of our own spirit. He also professes to know, that other human spirits outside and independent of his own exist, and of these spirits he has "notions" in his own spirit. Through or by means of these

subjective "notions" he professes to know objects, that
is, his own and other spirits outside and independent of
his own "notions" of them. But it is just as difficult, if
difficulty there be, to transcend his subjective "notions,"
so as to know "spirits" beyond and independently of these
"notions," as it is to transcend "ideas" to know objects
beyond those "ideas." If Berkeley then asserts, that he
knows only "ideas" and not the objects beyond these
"ideas," he should also have logically asserted that he
knows only "notions" and not substantial "spirits" beyond
and independently of his "notions." In other words if he
teaches that he knows "mountains," "tables," etc., only as
"ideas," he should consistently also teach that he knows
"his own spirit" and other "spirits" and "God" only as
mere "notions." All knowledge then, in his system, would
be confined to "ideas" and "notions," which, of course,
would be utter Phenomenalism to which Hume subsequently reduced his system, and not Pluralistic Immateri-
alism. Berkeley like Kant, was a pious man. He did not
wish God or spirits to be taken away from him. Yet we
are forced to admit that Hume was a keener logician than
Berkeley.

Let us now examine Berkeley's axiomatic dictum
which he applies to his "ideas," "*esse est percipi*," that is,
the being and existence of "ideas" consist in their being
perceived. Before "ideas" are perceived, they have no
being or existence, and when they cease to be perceived
they have no longer any being or existence. Is this axiom
true, when we consider Berkeley's system? We venture
to say that it is not, even if we should admit for the time
being Berkeley's explanation of the origin of his "ideas."
We must assume that the "mind or spirit" prior to its
perception of any of its "ideas" is, like all active agents
indifferent or in potency to perceive this "idea" or that.
That the spirit may perceive any particular "idea" its percipient activity must be awakened by some determinant
distinct from itself. What is this determinant? Berkeley
himself explains. He says: " 'ideas' (are) imprinted on
the senses (by God)." That is, there is an effect pro-

duced in the spirit by God which is now the term of its percipient activity or perception. The term, that is, the "idea," is *perceived*. In other words, the "idea" suffers the act of perceiving. That is the meaning of the passive voice—"being perceived." How, we may ask, could the "idea" suffer the act of being perceived or become the term of the percipient act, if the "idea" did not exist prior to, at least *by a priority of nature*, its perception. Trees are not felled, bones are not broken unless these objects exist before they suffer the action of being felled or broken. In like manner, if the "idea" had no being or existence before it is perceived then there would be nothing to suffer the action of being perceived.

Now, if the "ideas" must exist prior, by at least *a priority of nature*, before they can be perceived, then must they have an "esse" or being before they are perceived. But if the ideas have a being before they are perceived, then, it is not the happening or "suffering" of "being perceived" that constitutes their being, because their "being perceived" is posterior at least *by nature*, to their "esse" or being. Hence, the "esse" of an "idea" is not constituted by the facts of its being perceived. For it must exist before being perceived. And if it so exists, it must have a being independently of its being perceived. How would Berkeley explain the memory of "ideas" perceived in the past? Does God imprint the "idea" anew which we remember. Rather is there not some imprint or determinant left in the mind to decide the memory to recall this or that idea? If so that determinant is something. It has a being, and the being that is independent of the being which the remembered "idea" possesses, a being that is not imparted by actually "being perceived" by memory.

Lastly, when Berkeley asserts in the very first sentence of his Principles, that "ideas" (sensations or complexes of sensations) are the direct and immediate objects of human knowledge, he is begging the question for he is assuming the very first thing he ought to prove. This fundamental principle of Idealism, namely, that "ideas" are the direct object of perception, has been taken over from Descartes by Locke, Berkeley, Hume and Kant. But this principle of Idealism is not evident, as Berkeley says it is. If it were, the human race would be immediately, intuitively convinced of it, and would have accepted it without question as they accept other self-evident principles. But the human race does not accept it. Why? Because precisely it is not evident. Scholasticism replies to Berkeley's principle that "ideas" are not the direct objects of the senses, but the *means* by which we come directly to perceive the real objective external world.

CHAPTER IX

DAVID HUME (1711-1776)

LOCKE, Berkeley and Hume, the three classic names in the history of non-Catholic thought in England, Ireland and Scotland, are, in the marked individuality of their characters, representatives of their respective countries. Locke in speculations is the serious, sober-minded Englishman, Berkeley the spiritualistic Irishman, Hume the canny, sceptical Scotchman.

David Hume was born in Edinburgh, the Scottish Capital, on the 26th of April 1711. Hume says of his early years—"My family was not rich. My father, who posed for a man of parts, died when I was an infant, leaving me, with an elder brother and sister, under the care of our mother, a woman of singular merit, who, though young and handsome, devoted herself entirely to the rearing and educating of her children. My studious disposition and my industry gave my family a notion that the law was a proper profession for me, but I found an unsurmountable aversion for everything but the pursuit of philosophy and general learning."

His good mother is reported to have said of him, "Our Davie's a fine, good-natured crater, but uncommon wake-minded." Not the first time that the passion for philosophy has been mistaken for weakness of mind, and a sign for general good-for-nothingness.

On becoming of age, he found himself in possession of a small property, too small for honorable subsistence in England, but large enough to live in comparative comfort in France. He went to Rheims, near which was La Fleche, the alma mater of Descartes, where the Jesuit College and library was a great attraction to the studious youth, and there he passed several years in solitary study. It is strange that it was while living in the same surroundings in which Descartes began with doubt in order to arrive at certainty, Hume began with certainty to arrive at doubt.

It is strange, too, that it was while engaged in conversation with a Jesuit in La Fleche on the question of miracles, that Hume hit upon his famous argument against miraculous events, which he afterwards developed in his famous essay on that subject. While in France he prepared the manuscript of his "Treatise on Human Nature" which, on his return to England in 1737, received the finishing touches, and in 1739 the first two volumes of this treatise were published. The third volume on morals appeared the following year.

His "Essays" appeared in 1741, his "Political Discourses" and the "Inquiry Concerning the Principles of Morals" in 1752. The first volume of the work which was held the greatest title to his fame "The History of England" was published in 1754.

In 1747 he accompanied General St. Clair, as secretary, in the embassy to Vienna and Turin. He was in later life the librarian to the Faculty of Advocates in Edinburgh, which placed at his disposal a fine collection of books.

In presenting the main positions of Hume's philosophy we shall touch on four distinct headings.

I. He developed Locke's and Berkeley's principles to their ultimate logical conclusions. A brief explanation of these conclusions will serve the double purpose of bringing us to understand Hume, and of setting forth for all time the fatal flaws of both Locke's and Berkeley's principles.

Locke, you may recall, practically destroyed *substance* as an actually existing reality, when he said "substance is a *supposed, imagined, unknown* support of accidents." The inevitable and logical inference implied in this principle is, that neither material nor spiritual substances really exist. Hence though Locke *professed* to be a Realist, yet since substance was for him a mere mental creation—a "supposition," an "imagined," "unknown" something, bodies outside of us were a mere bundle or cluster of "qualities" existing alone without a subject or *qualified,*

and spirit or soul, and God could be nothing more than a
congeries of psychic or conscious states—"a stream of
consciousness" without any underlying, actually existing
substance to be conscious of them.

> "I am a stream of consciousness
> And on and on I flow.
> I cannot know myself at all
> There is no "I" to know.
> At morn I'm a psychic state, a feeling or emotion,
> And yet the stream of consciousness flows onward
> to the ocean."

It is true, as we have said, that Locke, who *professed*
Realism, considered that the material *qualities* of bodies
existed as realities, and the psychic or conscious states
as actually existing independently of any substantial soul
or spirit to sustain them. But Hume who was a keener
logician than Locke, reminded that typical English philosopher, that, at the very beginning of his philosophical
system, he adopted from Descartes the fundamental principle of Idealism, namely that "the mind hath no other
immediate object but its own ideas which it alone does or
can contemplate." If this is so, and if as Locke declared
all judgments consist only in "the perception of the agreement or disagreement of *ideas,* not of existing realities,"
then Hume insisted on logically legitimate grounds that
Locke could not know anything but his own subjective
ideas—a mere series of conscious phenomena, entirely
subjective, which represented no actually existing reality
outside of them. Cf. Treatise. I-p. 385 (Green). Locke
endeavored, through the "intervention of ideas" which he
dogmatically asserted were *representative* of realities beyond and independently of themselves, to demonstrate the
existence of objects outside his ideas, but Hume again insisted this attempted demonstration was a failure. Locke,
since he took his stand that the direct objects of his knowledge were subjective ideas never succeeded in making
the transcendence by a process of reasoning from his ideas

to actually existing realities. Were Locke, then, logically consistent, he should have been what Hume actually was, a Phenomenal Idealist, knowing nothing but conscious states of which nobody is conscious. For if substance whether spiritual or material, is only a creation of the mind and consequently not known as an actual existence, and if in addition the *idealistic principle* is also admitted and Locke maintained both of these positions, then nothing remains but psychic, subjective states without a subject,—a thought, for instance without a thinker, a feeling or emotion without anyone to feel or be moved. This is the system that Hume taught, and were Locke logical and consistent, this too should have been his system. Hence Hume deserves thanks for logically unfolding the implications enfolded in Locke's fundamental principles.

Hume was no less successful in reducing Berkeley's system also to Phenomenal Idealism. Berkeley, as we saw, denied the existence of material substances, declaring what ordinary people call bodies are only sensuous "ideas" within the mind, the existing essence (esse) of which consists in their being perceived (percipi,) so that what has a "percipi" exists, and what has no "percipi" does not exist. On the other hand the existing essence of spirits does not consist in "percipi," because they are not perceived as the "ideas" are, but rather spirits *perceive* the "ideas." The existing essence (esse) of spirits consequently, he says, consists in perceiving (percipere). That is, just as Descartes said that the essence of spirits or soul is *thought,* so Berkeley declares that the essence of spirits is *perception.* The whole range of existing objects then, is embraced in things that are either *perceived* (percipi) or are perceiving (percipere). Now as Dr. Coffey keenly remarks—"If all 'esse' is 'percipi,' 'pan-phenomenalism' or the 'Idealistic Phenomenalism of Hume,' is the inevitable consequence; if all 'esse' is *either* 'percipi' ('ideas') or 'percipere' (real 'minds' or spirits,') Berkeley fails to show how we can attain to a genuine knowledge of these latter as they really are, and not merely of 'perceptions,' 'appearances,' 'representations' of them." Epistem. II, p. 115. But if we can know "spirits" only as a congeries of "perceptions." "appearances," "representations," then is our knowledge of "spirits" also phenomenal, and hence all the objects both "ideas" and "spirits" which Berkeley knows are phenomena—that is, his system is reduced to Idealistic Phenomenalism like that of Hume. Indeed Berkeley himself, before he put the finishing touches to his "Principles," was, like Hume, a thorough going Phenomenal Idealist. For we find in his "Common Place Book" this remarkable passage—"Mind or spirit is a congeries of *perceptions*. Take away the perceptions and you take away the mind. Put the perceptions and you put the mind." If mind is only "a congeries of perceptions," then the mind is only a series of conscious states and in no sense a substantial existence. But Berkeley was a pious man, and so he exerted all the subtlety of his genius and the charm of his style to defend the substantial existence of his own, other spirits and God. Hume, however, made it manifest that Berkeley's principles logically and legitimately led to Phenomenalism. Berkeley admitted that his "ideas" were merely phenomena, mere misty phantoms, and his "spirits," being nothing more than a cluster of "perceptions," since "perceptions" constituted their essence, were likewise merely *phenomena, appearances*. It is true that Berkeley maintained that "there was *something* which perceived his 'ideas,' and this something I call mind, soul or spirit." But since he made "perceptions" the essence of this "something," it is impossible to conceive that "perceptions" are, or constitute, a percipient "something."

"Perception" is an act, and "the percipient" "something" or "spirit" is the agent that elicits the act. The act must be distinct from its agent or "spirit," and not as Berkeley conceived them identical. Moreover, the agent or "spirit" must exist prior to its own elicited act, by at least a *priority of nature*. Since the agent or "spirit" must, then, be distinct from its act, because it is a creature and not God, and must exist prior to the act elicited, the agent or "spirit" must have its own essence distinct from, and antecedent to, its act, or "perception." The "perception" is distinct from, and consequent to the "spirit" perceiving. "Perception" could not, then, be, as Berkeley maintained, the essence of the "something" or "spirit" that perceives.

But Hume did not critically examine both Locke's and Berkeley's gratuitous assumption of the Idealistic Principle, but pointed out by the crushing force of logic, that this principle could have no other issue, but Idealism. Neither did Hume critically examine Locke's practical denial of the *substantial* principle, nor Berkeley's principle that the essence of "spirit" was "perception," but made manifest that both these principles must logically lead to pure Pan-Phenomenalism. Thus did Hume, basing his conclusions upon the logical implications of the three aforementioned principles together with Locke's Sensism, give to the world his system of Phenomenal Idealism, which is really equivalent to Nihilism. Hume's universe was nothing else but a floating panorama of misty phantoms—"a phantasmagoria in the background of nothingness," as Huxley surmised, or "a stream of consciousness" as William James conceived the ego and the universe to be.

Hume's system of Phenomenal Idealism is most extraordinary; "impressions" without anything to be impressed; "ideas" without anybody "at home" to perceive them; psychical phenomena without a "psyche" or soul; ordinary words which are the abiding heritage of every language, such as personal pronouns, could have no meaning for Hume; there exist no subjects of rights or duties.

The present writer entertains the theory that Hume never intended that anybody should take him seriously. He said once to a friend—"When I play backgammon with my friends I am like other men." But Hume had no love for the English, whom he called "barbarians from the banks of the Thames." It may well be believed that his purpose was to poke fun at John Locke, the leading philosopher of England, and to show forth to the world with a canny touch of humor, the inanity of Locke's principles and his muddling inconsistencies, by unfolding the logical implications which were enfolded in Locke's philosophy, which neither Locke himself nor his contemporaries had sufficient logical acumen to perceive.

II. The second phase of Hume's philosophy that demands explanation is, how Hume accounts for three undeniable experiences which we are constrained to admit, but which this theory of Phenomenal Idealism cannot consistently explain. These facts of experience are: 1. In the first place, why is it that we are deluded into thinking that matter has a permanent existence outside of us? 2. Secondly, how does he explain *necessary truths*; and 3. thirdly, what account does he give of the common persuasion which all men have of the existence of *cause*, which is one of these necessary truths accepted by the human mind?

All three convictions, Hume asserts, are illusions. There is really no such thing as permanent existing substantial matter or soul, no such thing as objective necessary truths, no such thing as a principle of causation in Hume's philosophy. And the illusory convictions we entertain in the case of all three, come not from any objective reason we see in matter itself, because it does not, Hume declares with Berkeley, exist, or any objective ground for the real existence of necessary truths, or for the existence of the principle of causality, which determines our minds to view these truths as independent of our subjective sensuous experience. Hume was a thorough going Sensist and was honest enough not to "bootleg" as Locke did into the realm of his knowledge, supersensible or intellectual ideas distilled out of his own mind. Hume plainly declares that our minds consist of "impressions" by which he means the immediate experience of sense, and of "ideas" by which he means the paler copies of "impressions" recalled by memory. "You see, feel, taste, smell, hear. The objects in each case are merely *subjective* experiences. That is all. You have no other knowledge." (Royce—"Spirit of Modern Thought," p. 94.) Hume himself declares—"It is impossible for us to think of anything which we have not antecedently *felt*, either by our external or internal senses." "Did you ever see, taste, touch, or smell "necessary connection," or "causation?" You have never experienced, them, that is, you have no "impression" of these things. Neither can you have any "idea" of these things, for an "idea" to Hume is only a remembered "impression." Since "impressions" and "ideas" are purely subjective experiences, and they alone exist, the permanent and independent existence of matter and spirit, the conviction we have of the absolute and eternal existence of the objective truth of "causation" and of "necessary truths" are mere illusions.

1. How then, does Hume explain the illusion of the independent existence of material bodies outside of us? In the first place, when we experience an "impression" which we call matter, we spontaneously project this "impression" so vivid is it, and imagine it exists outside us. The *habit or custom*, which we gradually form by repeatedly *associating* the subjective "impression" with its objective projection as an extra-mental object creates the illusion that the object really exists even when unperceived. We do not avert to the fact that the "impressions" are only images of imagination, misty phantoms, "appearances" subjective "phenomena," which we imagine really exist, just as we happen to do in our dreams. We literally dream out our world.

The ineptitude of this explanation rests on two abnormal assumptions, first that we are always dreaming, that is, projecting outside of us as existing what are really only images of imagination, though we readily distinguish the incoherent, disorderly and irrational experiences of our dreams from the opposite qualities of the objects we perceive when awake. We do as a fact distinguish our dreaming from our waking moments, and when we do awake we realize the abnormality of our experiences while dreaming. The normal always precedes the abnormal. We could never know error unless we first knew truth; never know the abuse of something unless we first knew its use; what "negative" means unless we first knew what "positive" means. Hence "unless we had first perceived the actual world, we should have no dreams of the world of bodies, as the man blind from his birth who never saw colored objects, does not dream of colored objects." (Cotter-Epistem, p. 122.) Even if we grant for arugment's sake Hume's position, then was the very root of his nature in the simple exercise of his senses first abnormal and then normal, thus reversing the functioning of nature.

The second assumption is, that our senses by their *very nature* deceive us. That is, the purpose of nature (i.e. God) in endowing us with senses is irremediably to deceive us. Men are absolutely powerless, no matter what effort they make, to rid themselves of the primitive, intuitional report of their senses that bodies exist outside and independent of them. They are powerless to reconstruct a world in which nothing exists but projected, empty phantoms. To do so would mean that they divest themselves of their nature and adopt another. They may, by an effort, imagine for a short time that bodies are phantoms, but do what he may, no man can sustain for any prolonged period that imaginary attitude. We are constitutionally incapable of viewing the universe in this farfetched fashion.

"Naturam expellas furca, tamen usque recurrit." Hume must have arrived at his doctrine of "Phenomenalism" by trusting some cognitive faculty. To distrust he must have first trusted. Why did he trust one cognitive faculty of his nature and distrust the natural deliverances of his sense-faculties? All the faculties are endowments of nature. Were he consistent he should have distrusted all his cognitive faculties. If he did so, then universal scepticism would be the inevitable result. But universal scepticism is impossible. It defeats itself. For the most incorrigible sceptic who explicitly asserts "I cannot know anything for certain," in the same breath implicitly admits, "I am certain of this truth, I know nothing." Nature vindicates itself.

2. Hume's curious explanation to account for *necessary* and immutable truth is another peculiarity of his doctrine. Why is it that such as "2+2=4," "the whole is

greater than any of its parts," "a straight line is the shortest distance between two points" etc. are acknowledged by ordinary men, as absolute, immutable, that is, they *must* be what they are? Hume would answer, that we are so *accustomed to associate* together the "impressions" or "ideas" of the subjects and predicates of these propositions that we eventually form a *habit* or *custom* of so welding them together that we come to imagine that they must be what they are and cannot be otherwise, that the relations between their subjects and predicates are absolutely fixed and immutable. Hume, who is the real founder of the English Association School, would say that the *necessity* which we attribute to these truths is an illusion. For "necessity" is not an object of any sense, and since according to Hume's dictum—"It is impossible to go beyond sense-experience," we have no ground for asserting these truths are *necessary*.

The difficulty with this explanation is, why did we associate the "impressions" of the subjects and predicates of the propositions given above, the first time we experienced them? Was it a mere blind guess without the least justification arising from an intelligent understanding of the nature of two plus two and four etc? How did everybody hit upon the same guess? Guesses are not unanimous.

If habitual sensuous association between certain subjects and predicates could explain our conception of necessary truths, then why is it that we do not conceive the association between night and day, swans and white, robins and a red breast etc., as absolutely necessary. Surely after so long an experience of the co-existence of these facts, we ought to have formed the habit of necessarily associating them. But we do not. Hence mere association cannot explain necessary truths. The bond set up by association is, at best, subjective, a creation of the mind, whereas the connection between the subjects and predicates of necessary propositions is based on the nature of those subjects and predicates which the higher faculty of intellect perceives and discovers, but which it does not create.

3. Relying also on the same psychological effect of *habit* generated by repeated association, Hume explains our persuasion of the "principle of causality," that every *happening* is preceded by an *antecedent* which we call cause, in this way. We associate together, for instance, an *antecedent*, say the "sun" and the consequent "light," and because of our repeated observed experiences we form the *habit* of associating "sun" and "light" the one as something that precedes, the other as something that follows, and then come to regard the "sun" as the *cause* of "light." The idea of cause, then, is not determined by any actual, objective nexus or connection between "light" and the "sun," but arises from a *subjective habit* induced in the mind by associating the antecedent "sun" with the consequent "light." Hume's inference is, then, that in every case of what ordinary people call "causality," the antecedent has nothing to do with the production of the effect. The principle of causality, Hume would assert, is another case of illusion, because "causality" again is not an object of sense experience. What begins to be (effect) is *conjoined*, indeed, Hume would admit, with what we call in our delusion a cause, but they are not *connected* by any link of necessity. Hence Hume asserts "anything may be the cause (i.e. the mere conjoined antecedent) of anything else."

We may briefly summarize the philosophies of Locke, Berkeley and Hume thus: Locke, by practically eliminating substance from the realm of actual existence logically reduced all reality to Pan-Phenomenalism. Still Locke taught, though inconsistently indeed, that material primary qualities (common objects of sense) of bodies existed in the material universe—hence bodies, as conceived by Locke were merely a cluster of qualities. Secondary qualities of bodies (proper objects of sense) according to Locke existed not formally but only causally in bodies. Berkeley, a keener logician than Locke, not only denied outright the existence of material substances but also both the primary and secondary qualities of bodies in every sense, yet retained the substantial existence of "spirits"—his own

spirit, other spirits and God and their subjective "ideas."
Yet because Berkeley made "perceptions" the essence of
spirits, he therefore logically reduced spirits to a series of
conscious phenomena, and really should have been like
Hume, a Phenomenal Idealist. Hume tore away all the
illogical compromises of both Locke and Berkeley, and
denied not only material but also spiritual substances and
left nothing whatsoever of real existences, and made both
the spiritual and material world consist only of a flux
of appearances, phenomena, misty phantoms the mere
ghosts of things. Hume was a Nihilist in knowledge.
How could he know anything, when there was no Hume,
no "I" to know? Matter, spirit, immortality, God—all
are gone. Whether Hume was a Fideist, that is blindly
believed in those eternal verities, who can tell?

CHAPTER X

EMMANUEL KANT (1724-1804)

THE philosophy initiated by Descartes (1596-1650,) has, within the last three centuries, gradually developed into the many, varied and mutually contradictory systems which are historically known as "Modern Thought." Outside and apart from the multiplicity of these systems of "Modern Thought" stands "Scholasticism" alone and unique, not as a stereotyped, closed system, but ever capable of progressive development by assimilating whatever may have been discovered as reasonable and true by the founders of other systems. Error has many faces, truth has only one face.

In his inquiry into the origin of human knowledge and the nature of reality, Descartes made many useful suggestions. Hence the condemnation of his philosophical principles by the church was moderate—*"donec corrigantur."* Yet the following false principles of Descartes, which as a sad heritage he left to subsequent thinkers, developed into all the various systems of modern philosophy.

(1) His "Idealistic Principle," which, having been acquiescently accepted by all the Cartesians, by Locke, Berkeley, Hume and Kant, has poisoned all modern thought. This principle, and its corollary that "the mind can never transcend itself, so as to know anything external to itself," have opened the way to all the systems of the Idealistic schools, which have captivated the great majority of modern thinkers—cf. Case—"Physical Realism," p. 15.

(2) The absolute antithesis between soul and body, mind and matter and the consequent impossibility of their interaction—exaggerated Dualism—quickly developed, within the Cartesian School itself, into Occasionalism, Ontologism, Pre-established Harmony.

There is in the human mind, a natural propensity to

reduce what are disparate and disconnected to unity. This unity of human nature to which consciousness clearly testifies, has been effected by Scholasticism by maintaining that man is one complete substance constituted by two incomplete substances—body and soul. Spinoza brought about this unity in his theory of Pantheism, by conceiving "extension" which was Descartes' body, and "thought" which was Descartes' soul as two attributes of the one divine substance. The Spiritualists (Berkeley) reduced man to unity by destroying matter, and the Materialists, who were rampant in the eighteenth century in France, England, Dublin, Philadelphia, Kentucky, New York, unified man by destroying the soul.

(3) Descartes' "innate ideas," a form of ultra-intellectualism, are destructive of all objective reality and consequently of all science, because Innatism invalidly assumed that innate, subjective ideas had in the extramental world real objects corresponding to them, thus basing all science upon merely subjective ideas.

The spirit of innovation begun by Descartes now passed to England and inspired Locke, not, however, to acquiesce in all the principles of the distinguished extremist of France, but rather to set on foot a strong reaction against Cartesianism, and to found a new system historically known as Empiricism. Empiricism, even if it professes Realism, declares that the human mind can know such realities only as *directly* affect the senses, or as Scholasticism would express it, the human mind can know only the "proper" and "common" objects *per se* of the senses. This system practically denies or reduces intellect to sense. Like Positivism, Empiricism rejects from the range of human knowledge everything supersensible, and consequently denies Metaphysics. It is Sensism or Sensationalism pure and simple. This was the philosophy of Locke. If Locke admitted intellectual "ideas" and he seems to have admitted them, "substance," "cause," "necessity" etc., these intellectual ideas were not derived from objects of sense-experience, but were in Locke's system mere "creations of the mind." His position regarding objective realities that seemed to correspond to these "mental creations" was agnostic. This is why he insists that he never denied "substance" for example, neither did he admit that he *knew* the real existence of "substance." For, he declares that "substance" is the supposed, imagined, *unknown* support of qualities."

Locke, indeed, professed Realism. He declared that the "primary qualities" (common objects of sense) really existed, but since "substance" was a mere "creation of his mind," bodies outside of him were only a "cluster of primary qualities," while the "secondary qualities" (proper objects of sense) were formally subjective and only *causally* objective. But, since Locke also admitted the "Idealistic Principle" which he took over from Descartes, namely, that "the mind hath no other immediate object but its own ideas which it alone does or can contemplate" (Bk. IV-I. 1) this principle combined with his Sensism and with his theory that his pseudo-intellectual idea of "substance" was "a creation of his mind" logically leads to the conclusion that Locke should have been an Idealist. It is easy, then, to see, how, from the womb of Locke's Empiricism were born in due time, three new developments in the history of English thought—Berkeley's partial or objective Idealism, French, English and American Materialism, and Hume's Phenomenal Idealism. Berkeley was pious, and his purpose was religious, so he saved, or thought he saved, the substantial existence of his own spirit, other spirits and God, while he denied outright, basing this denial on the impossibility of Locke's Realism, that extra-mental bodily qualities *without a qualified* existed.

Hume now appears. With the development of Locke's inconsistencies by Berkeley into "Objective Idealism" and Locke's agnostic attitude towards all substances before his vision, Hume asked himself, assuming all Locke's principles—"What, then, can I know?" And he answered with the crushing forces of his keen logic, and we are inclined to think that his logic was correct, that "I can know nothing except a floating panorama of shadowy phantoms. If 'substance' is *unknown*, I cannot know that anybody exists who can know." This, of course, is the annihilation of all knowledge, complete universal scepticism—Nihilism. We may well doubt whether Hume accepted his own philosophy, or whether his whole system was not the outcome of a humorous academic exercise in logic with the view of exposing before the philosophical world the nihilistic implications enfolded in the muddling inconsistencies of Locke's Empiricism and in the pious compromise of Berkeley's partial Idealism. Hume denied not only material substance with Berkeley but also spiritual substance.

The drama of "Modern Thought," then, whose first act was the philosophy of Descartes, and the last act the philosophy of Hume, ended in the tragic death of all human knowledge. The contradictory philosophies of "Modern Thought" to Hume's day quarrelled among themselves unto their own utter destruction.

A new luminary in the philosophical world now appears—Emmanuel Kant (1724-1804). His avowed purpose was to refute Hume, and retrieve the fallen fortunes of bankrupt philosophy, and on lines of thought, and points of view which no other philosopher in history had hitherto conceived. Kant, then, inaugurates a new epoch in "Modern Thought." So important is Kant's system that Behn truly says:—"In our time a thinking person, who has not talked things over with Kant, cannot claim the title of philosopher"—("The Eternal Magnet," p. 382.) It will be interesting to study with what success Kant achieved his laudable purpose, as well as to visualise clearly the striking contrasts between his philosophy and that of Scholasticism. Who, then, was Kant?

Emmanuel Kant was born in Königsberg, Prussia, 22nd of April, 1724. His father who was a saddler, was of Scotch descent. His German mother, though upright and pious, was severe and exacting in character. Exceedingly regular in his habits, Kant led an uneventful and peaceful life and never left his native town. He smoked, drank his coffee, wrote, lectured, took his daily walk so regularly along the same route, that he was called by the townsfolk the clock of Königsberg. He rose at five, lectured in summer from 7-9, in winter from 8-10 A.M. The rest of the time he gave over to intense mental labor. A few intimate friends, with whom he discussed philosophical questions, were always present with him at dinner. His daily walk was then followed by lighter reading until bedtime.

He was sent early in life to the University, studied in addition to philosophy, mathematics, sciences, languages and cultivated literature, though his style always remained involved and somewhat uncouth. Like Descartes, Spinoza, Locke and Leibnitz, Kant never married. He died in his 80th year. DeQuincey in his "Miscellanies" gives an interesting account of his last days.

His great work was the "Critique of Pure Reason." Though it was the outcome of twelve years of meditation and study, the work itself he wrote in five months. At first the "Critique" attracted little attention, owing to the repulsiveness of its terminology and style. Its value was eventually discovered. All Germany sang its praises. Almost every university chair was soon filled by a Kantist. Numerous publications were poured from the press defending or attacking Kant's system.

The despair of philosophy which characterized Hume's philosophy "aroused" Kant (1724-1804) "from his dogmatic slumber." In youth he studied the philosophy of Wolff, a modification of Leibnitz's system, and taught it at Königsberg. At that time he admitted the existence of extended and non-extended substances, the essential difference between sensation and intellectual knowledge, the existence of things outside of and independent of the mind. To admit such truths is called by Kant "dogmatism."

In the course of time he began to doubt the validity of metaphysical science, i.e., *that REASON can put us in touch with REALITY.*

Kant, in his book, "The Only Possible Foundation for a Demonstration of God's Existence," (1763) rejected the cosmological and teleological arguments as proofs for the existence of an infinite God. Yet he asserted we can with certainty hold that God exists, though we are unable to demonstrate his existence. ("Pure Reason," Abbott, p. xxix.)

In his "Inquiry into the Principles of Natural Theology and Morals" (1764) he asserts that our knowledge of God and morality is derived rather from our internal personal experiences revealed by our CONSCIENCE than from any effort of speculative reason.

At the beginning of Kant's critical career, two outstanding systems of philosophy held sway, (1) a modified form of Leibnitz, which Kant had up to this time acquiescently accepted from his masters Wolff and Knutzen, and (2) English Empiricism. Scholasticism was, of course, ignored, especially by Kant, "who was," as Paulsen says, preeminently, "the philosopher of Protestantism." Under the scrutinising glance of his newly adopted "critical" attitude, both the first system which he now called "dogmatic," as well as the second, Empiricism, were found wanting by Kant. The simple reason was that neither of them, when submitted to "criticism" were adequate to account for the characteristic demands, as Kant understood them, of the mathematical and physical sciences, sciences which he, as well as all men of thought accepted as incontrovertibly true and certain. So Kant set about giving to the world a new philosophy, which he called the "Critical Philosophy," which he thought, would adequately explain all the demands of these sciences.

By "dogmatism" Kant understood any philosophy which professes to transcend the sphere of sense-experience without having previously justified this transcendence by a critical examination of the faculties of knowledge so as to explain the origin, the limits, the range and the possibility of human knowledge. By the "possibility" of human knowledge, Kant meant the conditions that are necessary in order that such knowledge may exist at all, and be free from contradiction. By "criticism," on the other hand, Kant meant an examination of the cognitive faculties with the view of determining the origin, the limits, the range and possibility of human knowledge. In other words, Kant critically examined and professed to answer the questions—"What can I know?"; "What ought I do?"; and "What may I hope for?"

Why, then, did Kant reject, as the result of his criticism, both the (1) Leibnitzian-Wolffian philosophy, the system of his early years, and (2) Empiricism as unsatisfactory? Because Kant clearly saw that all the judgments of the mathematical and physical sciences are (1) *necessary* and *universal*, and in addition to these characteristics these sciences are marked by another feature, namely, (2) *a continuous addition of new knowledge*, which cannot be explained, according to Kant's mind by any process of analysis, that is, by making explicit what may be implicit in their previously acquired store of judgments.

It is obvious that pure sense-experience or *Empiricism* can never account for the *necessity* and *universality* of scientific judgments. For "experience," as Kant says, "teaches us, no doubt, that something is so and so, but not that it cannot be different," that is, experience cannot tell us what *must* be so, that is, *necessarily* so. We experience only what is, as a fact, in each case, or what is contingent, that is, what may be different. And what may be different or contingent cannot be necessary— always the same, unchanged and unchangeable. Neither can Empiricism explain the genuinely universal judgments of science. Because as Kant again insists—"Experience never imparts to its judgments *true* or *strict*, but only *assumed* or *relative* universality." We can experience at best only *some* cases in the same field of thought, never *all* cases. From whatever source, the necessity and universality come to the judgments of science, these characteristics cannot come from Empiricism or experience alone. Hence pure Empiricism cannot explain scientific judgments.

It is true, however, that Empiricism can explain the second demand of science, namely, an increase of new knowledge. For new knowledge is expressed in "synthetic judgments," wherein the predicate is not seen to be contained in the subject, except as a fact revealed by experience (Empiricism). Hence Kant will not reject Empiricism altogether as a requisite in the explanation of scientific judgments. In fact, Empiricism, or knowledge through sense-experience alone will enter as an important contribution into Kant's theory of knowledge.

Kant also submits to "Criticism" his own previously accepted "Wolff-Leibnitzian" system which he now classified as "dogmatic." This system, based as it is, on *innate* ideas is known as Rationalism or "exaggerated intellectualism." Corresponding to these innate ideas, it dogmatically assumed that real objects existed outside and independently of these ideas. These innate ideas of Leibnitz were indeed necessary and universal. They were fixed, unchangeable, absolute, because, in accord with the peculiar doctrine of Leibnitz, they represented a world that was the best possible which God could create. Since then, in this system, science was based on innate ideas, it logically follows that all the judgments of science were purely analytic judgments arrived at by an analysis of these innate ideas. If the innate ideas themselves were necessary and universal so were all judgments arrived at by simply unfolding or making explicit what was already enfolded or implicit in these ideas. However, though the Innatism of Leibnitz could explain the necessity and universality of scientific judgments, yet it could not explain the second feature which Kant demanded for science, namely, an increase of new knowledge. Because, to the mind of Kant, the mere analysis of ideas doesn't add one jot of new knowledge to what is already enfolded or implicit in the original innate ideas, any more than the mere counting of the money in your pure increases the amount of money already contained in it. Hence Kant rejected both Empiricism *alone*, and "innate ideas" *alone*, as inadequate to captain the judgments of the mathematical and physical sciences.

The outcome, then, of Kant's criticism of the Innatism of Leibnitz and of English Empiricism was that while the innate ideas or Rationalism of Leibnitz could explain the necessity and universality of scientific knowledge, it could not explain the demand for a further increase of knowledge, while Empiricism could explain the further increase of scientific knowledge, but could not account for the elements of necessity and universality of scientific knowledge. The sequel, however, will show that Kant will include in his theory of scientific knowledge both an element of Empiricism or sense-experience, and also an element of Innatism, though the meaning which he will attribute to both these elements will differ from the ordinary meaning which is attached to these terms. Kant's theory of knowledge will then appear to be a compromise between his modified meaning of Empiricism or sense-experience and his modified meaning of innate ideas. He will profess to account for the element of necessity and universality characteristic of all scientific judgments by a certain form of Innatism, and the element of variety and increase of knowledge in the sciences by a modified form of sense-experience or Empiricism—so that he will maintain that the human mind cannot form any scientific judgment unless it contains at the same time an intellectual element derived from his modified form of innate ideas and a sense element derived from sense-experience. In a word, Kant's system of scientific knowledge will appear to be a "via media" between Empiricism, which will supply a sense-element, and a modified Innatism which will supply an intellectual element to such knowledge.

Let us now examine how Kant, in order to explain the origin of the two essential elements in scientific judgments, namely the (1) element of necessity and universality, and the (2) element of an increase or amplification of knowledge, makes use of "sense-experience" (Empiricism) *to add something new to our knowledge,* and utilizes also a modified form of "innatism" (Rationalism) to impart to our knowledge, over and above an increase of knowledge, the feature of *necessity and universality,* and thus render our knowledge truly scientific. This Empirico-Intellectualism of Kant must be carefully distinguished from the Empirico-Intellectualism of Scholasticism.

(1) Knowledge is perfected in judgment. The judgments, then, that embody knowledge are of two kinds—(1) Analytic and (2) Synthetic. In analytic judgments the predicate is already contained, at least implicitly in the subject, as "bodies are extended," "a circle is round." Such judgments are, indeed, *necessary* and *universal*, a priori, but in Kant's view, these judgments do not amplify our knowledge. They lack, therefore, one of the requisites demanded by Kant to constitute scientific knowledge. We shall afterwards see the difference between Kant's and the Scholastic interpretation of analytic judgments.

(2) In "synthetic judgments" the predicate is outside the notion of the subject. They do add something to, or amplify our knowledge of the subject. They are of themselves based on experience—*a posteriori*, and hence contingent, that is, they lack necessity and universality. They tell us what is, not what must be. Hence of themselves they are not scientific. Kant admits that there are some synthetic judgments wholly synthetic and contingent, because they express an individual, and sometimes a personal fact, and hence are lacking the feature of necessity and universality, as for instance, "I have a toothache," "The United States is a republic." Hence, they are not scientific.

But there are other synthetic judgments, Kant maintains, in which the feature of necessity and universality is present. And since they possess both the requisites demanded by science, as Kant understands science, these synthetic judgments are truly scientific, and they alone are scientific. Examples of such judgments are proposed by Kant, as, for example, the mathematical judgments— "A straight line is the shortest distance between two points;" "7+5=12;" and in metaphysics,—"Whatever begins to be must have a cause." In these judgments Kant maintains, that the predicates are not contained in the subjects, but that the predicate tells us something over and above what can be derived from the subject by analysis. They are not analytic judgments Kant strenuously maintains. They are truly synthetic, therefore, they amplify our knowledge. At the same time they are admittedly necessary and universal, hence "a priori." They are strictly scientific judgments. Kant consequently defines science as a collection of *synthetic judgments a priori*. How then are "synthetic judgments a priori," that is, judgments that are at the same time "*a posteriori*" because *synthetic,* hence experiential, and "a priori" because they are *necessary* and *universal,* a feature that cannot be *given* by experience, formed? What are the conditions of their existence. This is the whole problem of Kant's "Critique."

Kant, now, in order to thoroughly explore the working of the cognitive faculties with a view to discovering how they work, so that they secure the presence in all scientific judgments of those two essential features—(1) the feature of "synthesis" which imparts to science *an increase of knowledge* and the (2) feature of *necessity and universality* which makes them objective, divides the faculties of knowledge into

a.—Sensibility (i.e., outer and inner senses and
    imagination.)

b.—Understanding

c.—Reason

and institutes a searching criticism of each.

a.—*Sensibility*—In the first part of the "Critique of Pure Reason" which is known as the *"Transcendental Esthetic,"* he critically analyses the conditions of sense knowledge. As the outcome of this criticism, Kant declares that every object of both outer and inner sense-perception, or of "sense-intuition" as Kant calls "perception," is an amalgam of two distinct elements.

In the case of the external senses, there is the *impression* or *sensation* (i.e. an impression of some "proper object" of the outer sense) passively received, and caused, in some mysterious way by what Kant calls "The-thing-in-itself" or *noumenon* which he postulates as existing outside and independently of the mind. This impression or sensation is the first element of an object of the outer sense.   Mark well that Kant maintains that "the-thing-in-itself" (noumenon) is an *unknown* something. He does not know whether it is one, or many, a substance or accident etc.   One predicate alone he affirms of it, namely, existence.   It exists.   This "thing-in-itself" is the only remnant which Kant retains from his former system of Realism, which he professed to admit during his pre-critical or "dogmatic" years.

There is also in every object of "sense-intuition" a second element, namely, an element of *necessity and universality* distinct from the mere impression.   This second element cannot arise from the mere impression, because the impression is an individual experience, and necessity and universality, as was previously explained, cannot be *given* or produced by experience, which always gives only an individual concrete something.   This element of necessity and universality comes *from out the mind itself*, where it is lying unconsciously before or "a priori" to all experience, and is, in case of the external senses, the "a priori form" of "*space*," in the case of the internal senses, "time."   When the "a priori form" of *space*, coming from out the mind, superimposes itself upon the "impression" of the outer senses, then have we an object of "sense-intuition," an object, however, which does not actually exist outside the mind, but which is a "phenomenon," a subjective phantom before the mind.   For, according to Kant, we can never know anything but "phenomena," never a thing that exists independently of the mind.   It cannot be but a *subjective* phenomenon, because the element of experience in it—the "impression," which is called the "*matter*" of the object of a sense-intuition, is subjective, and the element of necessity and universality which is called the "form" coming as it does from the mind, is likewise *subjective*.   Hence the object before the mind, composed as it is by subjective elements, is wholly subjective.   *Yet Kant always calls such an object really objective.*   Because the term "*objective*" always means for Kant, whatever contains a necessary and universal element.   For such an element is the same for all human minds as they are at present constituted. Kant in his writings habitually ascribes to philosophical terms a meaning quite different from that which they traditionally bear.

"Space" and "time" since they come not from experience but from out the mind, have no real existence outside of us. Ordinary people very positively think *space* and *time* really exist. But Kant would say this is a naive illusion.

The reason that Kant gives for maintaining that "space" and "time" are necessary and universal elements in every phenomenon of outer and inner sense respectively is the fact that willy nilly we cannot possibly think of any object of the external senses without thinking of them in "space." We *must* think it so. Nor can we think of any objects of the internal senses without thinking of them as succeeding to some other object that went before—Consciousness of succession is always and necessarily present, that is, we must think them in *time*.

Throughout his whole system, Kant has distorted the part played by reality and the mind in the genesis of truth. Instead of making the reality mould and shape the mind so that the mind be conformed to reality, Kant makes the mind mould or shape reality, so that the reality may be conformed to the mind. Hence Kant would say, "a thing is because we think it is, not that we think it is, because it is, independently of our thinking." It is only God could do what Kant says he does. Kant usurps the place of God in the generation of truth. It is the old heresy of the garden of Eden over again—"You shall be as gods."

b.—*Understanding*—The criticism of the Understanding is found in Kant's "Transcendental Analytic." In this part of his "Critique" Kant professes to reveal the "a priori forms" lying unconsciously ready in the understanding antecedently to all experience, and without which we could not form any *concepts* of the understanding at all. These "a priori forms" of the understanding, which are *twelve* in number, are the necessary conditions for the formation of concepts, just as "space" and "time" were the necessary conditions for our perceiving "phenomena" by the senses.

The most important of these "a priori forms" or "Categories" of the intellect are "cause" and "substance." The twelve intellectual "a priori forms" correspond to the "Predicaments" or "Categories" of Aristotle and Scholasticism. But whereas the Aristotelian categories which, as concepts, represent the highest classes into which all *reality* is divided, and are *founded upon reality and give knowledge of reality*, Kant's categories are only purely empty concepts *not founded* at all on reality nor do they give us any information of reality. These "a priori forms" of the understanding are all *universal* as well as necessary concepts, that is, they impart as *forms* to the matter upon which they are imposed universality and necessity.

Now the "matter" upon which these "a priori forms" of the understanding are superimposed is the "phenomenal objects" of "sense-intuition." These "phenomenal objects" of sense are already an amalgam of "matter,"— the *sense-impression* caused by the "noumenon" plus the "a priori sense forms" of "*space*" and "*time*." Why are these "a priori forms of the understanding" imposed upon the phenomena of sense? Because each of these sensuous phenomena are pictured by the imagination as either a *substance*, a *cause*, as *one* or *many* etc., and when they are so imaginatively pictured, the appropriate "a priori form of the understanding" pops forth from "the fairy rath of the mind" where live these "a priori forms" and attaches itself to the sensuous phenomenon and then we *necessarily* and *universally* are forced to think that such a sense-phenomenon is a *substance*, such another a *cause*, an *accident*, one or many etc. But in *reality*, of course, they are no such thing, for these "a priori forms" give us no insight into reality. Kant was a strict "Conceptualist" and in no way a "Moderate-Realist" as Aristotle and the Scholastics are.

The following is a list of Kant's twelve "a priori forms" or "Categories" of the Understanding—

   I. Of Quantity
      (a) Unity
      (b) Plurality
      (c) Totality
  II. Of Quality
      (a) Affirmation
      (b) Negation
      (c) Limitation
 III. Of Relation
      (a) Substantiality
      (b) Causality
      (c) Reciprocity
  IV. Of Modality
      (a) Possibility
      (b) Existence
      (c) Necessity

The objects of the understanding, just as the objects of sense, are all phenomena. Hence science tells us nothing of reality. We know nothing but phenomena, appearances, phantoms. This is the answer to his own question—"What can I know?" We dream out our world. We cannot even know ourselves (the Ego) except as a phenomenon. The real Ego is as unknown as "the-thing-in-itself." "I do not know myself at all." Because the real Ego, if it exists at all, is a substance." But Kant's "substance" is an "a priori form" that has nothing corresponding to it in reality. Kant eliminated from the sphere of reality "substance" and "cause." And notice, that an "a priori form" can only be applied to "matter" which has a subjective sense-element. And because the objects of metaphysics are above the sphere of sense, that is, they have no sense element, Kant eliminated Metaphysics from the sphere of knowledge. Kant was really, like Locke, a Sensist, that is, a Subjective Sensist. Kant was also a thorough-going Idealist. Were it not for that mysterious thing-in-itself (noumenon) which he saved from the wreck of reality as *existing* but *unknown*, Kant would have been as far as speculative reason is concerned, as radical a "Phenomenal Idealist" as Hume was.

The final answers which Kant has given to the first question, "What can I know," which he proposed to solve in his 'critical philosophy' are appalling in their destructiveness. He professes to *know* nothing that *is*, whether in the physical world without, or the psychical world within us. In both worlds he knows only what *seems* or *appears* to be, *phenomena* in his altered meaning of that term, and phenomena alone. "Things-in-themselves" as realities independent of the knowing mind are enveloped within the impenetrable darkness of the *unknown*. Knowing as an activity of mind, as Kant conceived it, is not an exploring and then a discovering of realities just as they are, independently of their being known, but knowing is rather the reconstructing or the remaking anew the "objects" of his knowledge, which, when thus reconstructed in the knowing process, are not things as they really *are*, but dream-like phantoms, images of the imagination, effigies or substitutes of real things projected before the mind—appearances, phenomena. Hence all the objects which Kant professed *to know* are subjective creations of his sensibility and understanding. What of reason in Kant's theory of knowledge? Does reason put Kant in touch with reality or things-in-themselves or noumena?

Deeply set in the rational nature of every man is the propensity ("Curiositas" of Aristotle) to endeavour if possible to account for each contingent phenomenon as it comes under observation by some previous cause. If this cause is again found to be contingent, and hence incapable of accounting for itself, it must be again explained by some further cause. The retrogressive process of reasoning is perseveringly pursued until the ultimate cause of the whole series of phenomena is discovered— a cause that has no other cause, a cause that is necessary and final in its own right. Thus are all contingent phenomena whether of the outer world, of the physical, or the inner world of the psychical order reduced to unity.

Taking a survey, then, of the entire universe of his

phenomenal experiences, Kant obviously finds that they are divided into the following departments:—

(1) The manifold psychical phenomena of consciousness.

(2) The manifold physical phenomena of the material world.

By a supreme effort of Reason, Kant reduces the first series of phenomena to unity by attributing them ultimately to one root cause—the "Ego." The second series of phenomena he likewise reduces to unity by attributing them to the "Cosmos." But the "Ego" and the "Cosmos" are in themselves contingent. To bring the "Ego" and the "Cosmos" again into unity, Kant seeks an ultimate cause, and discovers that it is "Theos" (God). Thus did Kant, conforming to an irresistible urge of human reason, reduce all the phenomena he professed to know to ultimate unity.

But does Kant admit that the "Ego," the "Cosmos" and "God" are known to him as real existents? He cannot, because none of these ultimates is a phenomenon, which alone for him is an object of knowledge. They are not phenomena because every phenomenon is a composite made up of an "a priori form" that comes from the mind and a basic, subjective sense-element or a subjective sense impression (matter) caused by the unknown noumenon. But since the "Ego," or "Cosmos" or "God" as objects of thought have no sensuous or empirical element to constitute their "matter," they cannot be known even as phenomena. Even if he did know them as phenomena, they would still be but mere shadows or appearances of real existents, not real existents in themselves. Neither can Kant know them as noumena, for in his theory all noumena are unknown. But while they cannot be known either as phenomena or noumena, Kant insists that we must *think* them. The "Ego," therefore, the "Cosmos" and "God," which we *cannot know* but *must think* of are mere "ideas," empty of all existing reality. In his own technical terms, he calls the "Ego" the psychological, the "Cosmos" the cosmological and the "idea of God" the

theological "idea." Kant does not deny the real or noumenal existence of any one of these "ideas." He simply
asserts we *cannot know* them though we must *think* them.
Kant is consequently agnostic in his attitude towards the
real "Ego," the real "Cosmos" and the reality of God.
Such is the issue of Kant's criticism of "pure reason."
It is appalling to contemplate the ruin which Kant has
made of the deliverances of reason, which, among the
cognitive faculties, has been looked upon throughout the
ages as the noblest prerogative of man.   Luther in the
sixteenth century and the development of Locke's Empiricism at the hands of Spencer in the nineteenth century taught the same Agnosticism.   No wonder Paulsen
calls Kant "the philosopher of Protestantism."   Agnosticism, though not the theoretical Atheism of present day
Russia, is, nevertheless, practical Atheism.

Did Kant rest satisfied with this practical Atheism of
despair, which renders all religion impossible?   How
could Kant believe in God, whom he confesses he does not,
and cannot know?   What power is left him to penetrate
the dark metaphysical region of the unknown and there
discover once more the freedom of the will, the immortality of the soul and the actual existence of God?   For this
achievement his "sensibility" is obviously inept and his
understanding and reason have already been found wanting.   To find a way out of this agnosticism, into which
his philosophy had ultimately developed, Kant must have
been at his wits' end.   In Kant's youth his pious German
mother fostered in his soul her religion of Pietism, and it
may well be, that the natural bent of his character reechoed the religious traditions of his paternal Celtic,
Scotch ancestry.   We may well believe that it was these inherited pious instincts which so revolted against his Agnosticism, that inspired the following protest—"The just
man may say *I wish* that there be a God; I insist upon it;
I will not have my faith taken from me."[1]   Kant flatters
himself for having discovered a new way to bring God

---

[1]Donat, Freedom of Science, p. 44.

into existence, which no thinker of the ages ever dreamt of. This was the way of his will: "*I wish* that God exists; I will that God exists, and lo! as if by magic, God once more *is*. This blind wish of the will—a naked "*volitum*" without a "*praecognitum*"—is what Kant calls faith, not, of course, faith in the Catholic sense. How could Kant even will, when he knows not his will or anything else as a real existent? His whole philosophy is a juggling with phenomena, empty of real existence, as are his "ideas," of Reason. It was to make room for this kind of blind faith that Kant boasted—"I have destroyed reason to make room for faith." Thus did Kant separate the allied faculties of reason and will and establish the illegitimate supremacy of will over reason. Man is no longer a rational but a willing animal. Law is no longer an ordination of reason but a decree of the dictatorial power of will which seems analogous to the modern systems of governments which rule by the decrees of dictators. This blind supremacy of will over reason seems to suggest, if it does not approve, tyranny.

It is impossible to understand how the will can become a talismanic power to bring forth into actual existence what is professedly unknown to exist. How can volition become "cognition" and "I wish" become "I know?"

In his "Critique of Practical Reason" which is another name for his will, Kant professes to have discovered a guide to conduct, which he calls the "Categorical Imperative." Who imposes on me this command which implies an "ought" and obligations to obey? Myself. Myself commands myself. How could myself, even if Kant professed to know the noumenal self, which he does not, who is equal to myself, command myself? Command supposes a superior and I am not superior to myself. Yet Kant teaches that if we obey any external authority even God, we act immorally. Hence, when we repeat the Lord's prayer we must say, if we admit Kantian morality, not "Thy will be done," but "my will be done."

An adequate and detailed examination and criticism

of Kant is beyond the scope of this little book. Balmes, Coffey, Jeannière, Walker and Pritchard may be consulted with profit.

Kant's doctrines are destructively opposed to Catholicism. His teaching has been condemned by Popes Leo XIII and Pius X. His great work, "The Critique of Pure Reason" was placed on the Index, 11th of June, 1827. Inconsistent with Catholic teaching are (1) Kant's Metaphysical Agnosticism, which declares his ignorance of all things as they really are; (2) his Moral Dogmatism, which declares the supremacy of will over reason, thereby making blind will without the guidance of reason the rule of action; (3) his giving to religious dogma merely a symbolic signification; (4) diametrically opposed to scholastic teaching and the common sense of mankind is Kant's theory of knowledge which makes mind and thought the measure of reality rather than making reality the measure of the mind and thought. Kant maintains that things are so because we must think them so, not that we must think them so because they are really so independently of our thinking them. The reversal of the order of thought and reality, Kant calls his "Copernican Revolution" in his theory of knowledge.

Appendix

INTIMATIONS OF KANT IN THE PHILOSOPHY
OF LOCKE*

RARELY if ever do we find in the history of thought any philosopher who sets forth explicitly and logically all the implications involved in his own fundamental principles. So short is life and so feeble is human intellect, that centuries may sometimes intervene between pronounced premises and their ultimate consequences. The combined intellectual power, for instance, of a Geulincx, a Malebranche, a Leibnitz and a Spinoza, was requisite to develop the implications in the seed-principles of Descartes.

This patient process of intellectual incubation may be also illustrated by the discussion of the subject that has been chosen for this paper—"The Intimations of Kant in the Philosophy of Locke."

In this declaration that Kant's theory of knowledge was, to a certain extent, embryonic in Locke's principles, we do not mean that Kant's complete teachings are logically implied in Locke's system. The "categorial imperative" of Kant seems wholly foreign to Locke's mind, and between the utilitarian ethics of Locke and the autonomous ethics of Kant, there seems to be no implicit logical connection. We shall, therefore, limit our investigations to Kant's speculative philosophy alone. Nor do we intend to set forth an exposition and criticism of either Locke's or Kant's theories of knowledge. We shall suppose that the reader is already well acquainted with both of these systems. But what we do propose to make manifest is, that Locke, while muddling through to explain the origin

---

*Paper read at the Third Annual Meeting of the American Catholic Philosophical Association held at Holy Cross College, Worcester, Mass., Dec. 27-28, 1927.

Reprinted from Thought, March, 1928. With permission of the Editor.

and content-value of certain traditionally accepted elements of human knowledge, with the view of fitting them
in with his assumed principles, actually stumbled upon,
and consequently anticipated, three of the outstanding
features of Kant's theory of speculative knowledge, viz:

1. Kant's Idealism;
2. Kant's Phenomenalism;
3. Though the assertion may seem daring, yet we
contend, that Locke also suggestively anticipated that
feature which is considered uniquely Kantian—the famous
"a priori forms."

Of course, like most pioneer efforts, Locke left those
anticipations of Kant in a somewhat crude, covert and
nebulous form. But Kant was, on his father's side, raci-
ally a Scotchman. No doubt the subtlety of his Celtic
and the constructive genius of his German nature contributed to his definitely crystallizing Locke's rather
amorphous theories, and to his giving them a respectable
position in philosophical society, by dignifying them with
the titles of a learned and polysyllabic terminology.

I

We shall now endeavor to establish by proof our triple
contention. In the first place, should Locke's theory of
knowledge, from a strictly logical point of view, have
issued in idealism, just as we know that the outcome of
Kant's speculative system was, generically at least, idealistic? We say "from a strictly logical point of view,"
because everybody knows that Locke was, by profession,
and repeated assertion, a realist, that is, he professed to
know the actual existence of objects and some of their
qualities outside and independent of his "ideas." Yet
this dogmatically asserted realism of his, as we hope to
show, outran the evidence of his own explicit principles
or premises. Hence Locke's realism can only be accounted
for, by his native English common sense, which unscrupu-
lously broke through the barriers of consistence and logic,
and thereby enriched his final realistic conclusion by a
surplusage of assumptions which were not guaranteed by

the implications of his original and explicitly declared principles.

Should Locke, then, logically have been an idealist, that is, should the logical outcome of Locke's principles limit the objects of human knowledge to a floating panorama of subjective ideas or psychical appearances of "he knew not what," following one another, "like," as William James would say, "so many beads without a string," or as Huxley would have it, "a phantasmagoria on the background of nothingness?" We maintain that Locke's philosophy, when stripped of the incrustations of its many contradictions and inconsistencies, and when the residual kernel is reduced to logic, as Berkeley partly, and Hume fully, accomplished, will be found to be idealistic as Kant's speculative philosophy was idealistic.

This idealism of Locke we now proceed to prove, firstly from the internal evidence of his explicitly declared principles, and secondly from the authoritative testimony of the philosophers of his own English school.

Before entering into his inquiry, which was the origin of ideas and the limitations of human knowledge, Locke in his "Essay" dogmatically assumed, without examination or criticism, the well-known idealistic postulate of Descartes, just as Kant uncritically assumed it, viz., that the direct and immediate objects of knowledge are never realities actually existing independently of the mind, but his own subjective ideas, objects, therefore, intramental, without any objective value. The world of direct and immediate knowledge is, therefore, never *without* but *within* him. This principle Locke explicitly asserts in the following passage. He says:[1]

"But before I proceed on to what I have thought on this subject, I must here in the entrance beg pardon of my reader for the frequent use of the word "*idea*," which, I think, serves best for whatever is the *object* of the understanding when a man thinks. I have used it to express whatever is meant by *phantasm, notion, species,* or what-

---

[1]Essay, Introd., 8. (Unless otherwise noted the italics are Locke's own.)

ever it is which the mind can be employed about in
thinking."

In this passage Locke abandons the traditional meaning of the term "idea," and uses it in the widest generic
sense, that embraces in its extension sensuous perception,
sensuous images of the imagination or phantasms, as well
as intellectual "notions" or "species."

In several other passages in his "Essay" Locke insists
that the objects which immediately and directly terminate
his perceptive gaze are always subjective ideas. He is
always directly looking inwards, never outwards. Locke
writes:[2] "Since the mind of man, in all its thoughts and
reasonings, hath no other object but his own ideas, it is
evident that our knowledge is only conversant about
them." This passage is a plain and explicit declaration of
Idealism. If "the mind has no other objects but its own
ideas," and if "it is only conversant about them," then,
ideas and ideas alone can be known. If "the mind is *only*
conversant about ideas," then would it be a contradiction
to say, that it is conversant about any objects apart
from ideas.

Furthermore, Locke's explicit and formal definition of
knowledge, which he emphasizes by italics, justifies logically his inclusion among idealists. He states:[3] *"Knowledge* then seems to me to be nothing but *the perception
of the connection of, and the agreement, or disagreement
and repugnancy of any of our ideas*. In this alone it
consists."

Now what is the logical consequence of Locke's explicitly declared principle that the direct and immediate
objects of all knowledge are never objects outside and independent of the knowing subject, but "ideas" wholly
within the percipient subject? The fatal consequence is
this. If "the mind hath no other objects but its own
ideas," if "our knowledge is *only* conversant about ideas,"
and if knowledge, which, in its perfection, is found in
judgment, "is nothing but the perception of the agreement

[2]Bk. IV, Ch. I, 1.
[3]Bk. II, Ch. I, 2.

or disagreement of any of our ideas," and if "knowledge consists alone in this," then are ideas, or psychical happenings objectively valueless, and the only materials the mind possesses wherewith to work, and to construct all its judgments and therefore all its knowledge. Hemmed in within a walled fortress enclosing only ideas, Locke would be forever precluded from experiencing anything of the outside world, and absolute subjectivism could not be avoided. Locke's mind could never transcend itself to know anything outside itself, and he would be doomed forever to contemplate, like a maniac, his own subjective ideas.

Locke, we know professed to be a "representative realist." But how could he legitimately plead that his ideas, on the assumption that they alone were the direct objects of his knowledge, are yet representative of actually existing objects outside themselves? For, how could he ever know that any image by its nature portrays a certain actually existing object, unless he knows or somebody else knows, directly the existing object that image represents? But to know directly such an object would be a surrender to direct perception, which Locke has explicitly repudiated in several passages, as for instance when he says:—"the mind has no other objects but its own ideas."

Again, to re-present means to present anew or once more. How could he know that an actually existing object is presented once more to his mind, unless he was directly aware of that object at its first or previous presentation?

Locke himself confirms the impossibility of establishing through what he calls "the intervention of ideas" which are first and directly known, the actual existence of bodies outside of him. For he remarks:[4] "Having the idea of anything in our mind, no more proves the existence of that thing, than the picture of a man evidences his being in the world, or the vision of a dream makes thereby a true history."

---

[4] Bk. IV, Ch. XI, 1.

To give full credit to Locke, he saw clearly that the pressure of evidence, furnished by his own admitted principles, pointed to Idealism, and we know he made desperate efforts to transcend his own subjective ideas, with the view of establishing the actual existence of outward objects. For instance he says:[5] "It is evident that the mind knows not the things immediately but only through the intervention of ideas it has of them." This passage is ambiguous, and may, as every Scholastic knows, be interpreted in a true sense. But this passage taken in connection with Locke's previous statement obviates such an interpretation. Then, Locke continues:

"Our knowledge, therefore, is real only so far as there is a *conformity* between our ideas and the reality of things. But what shall be here the criterion? How shall the mind, when it perceives nothing but its own ideas, know that they agree with things themselves? *This . . . seems not to want difficulty.*" (These italics ours.)

To this I answer[6] that "if our knowledge of our ideas terminates in them, and reach no farther, where there is something further intended, our most serious thoughts will be little more than the reveries of a crazy brain."

Locke in the foregoing passages sets forth fairly, squarely, honestly the epistemological problem that has tormented the "representationists" and "reasoned realists" from the days of Descartes to the present time— "how shall the mind, when it perceives nothing but its ideas, know that they agree with things themselves?" Of course it is a spurious problem, that would never have arisen, had not Descartes maneuvred the thought of his time into a false position, that became the occasion of victory for modern Idealism.

Did Locke succeed in solving his famous problem in favor of Realism—"How shall the mind, when it perceives nothing but its own ideas, know that they agree with things themselves?" We answer, that Locke, though he exhausted all the resources of his ingenuity to establish

---

[5]Bk. IV, Ch. IV, 3.
[6]Ibd., 2.

the existence of objects outside of him, yet failed to establish conclusively his professed Realism.

In the first place, he tiresomely repeats the fallacy of "begging the question," that is, in his very statement of the question at issue, he naively assumes the answer. He asserts, for instance:[7] "There can be nothing more certain than that the idea *we receive from an external object* (italics ours) is in our minds. This is intuitive knowledge." Of course, "there can be nothing more certain," because it is intuitive that the *idea as an idea* is in the mind. But that is not the question proposed by Locke, when he asked, "How shall the mind, when it perceives nothing but its own ideas, know that they agree with things? No solution of that problem could be arrived at by Locke who knows nothing "but his own ideas." Intuitively he is aware only of his own ideas, which are only one term of the equation between his ideas and things. So, to avoid the difficulty of demonstrative proof, Locke, with the effrontery of a mendicant, boldly "begs the question" by assuming that "we receive our ideas from external objects."

The fact is that Locke flirted with the direct perception of objects outside of him. But to state explicitly "Perceptionism" in the seventeenth century, dominated as that period was by Descartes, and the subjectivism of Protestantism, would be a reversal to discredited Scholasticism. Yet it seems to me, that in the following passage, wherein Locke endeavors to prove the genuine objectivity of his ideas on the basis of the "vividness" of sense ideas, when compared with the languid paleness of ideas of imagination and memory, he, in contradiction to his principle, that he knew nothing but his ideas, either implicitly admitted direct perception, or if he did not, then his statement will serve as another glaring example of "begging the question." He writes:[8] "For I ask anyone, whether he be not invincibly conscious to himself of a different perception when he *looks on the sun by day* and thinks of it by night;

[7]Bk. IV, Ch. II, 14.
[8]Ibid.

when he *actually tastes wormwood*, or *smells a rose*, or only thinks of that savour or odour?" (All italics ours.) What do the expressions, "looks at the sun by day," actually tastes wormwood" and "smells a rose," plainly mean except direct perception of those objects? But if he does not mean that he perceives the "sun," the "wormwood" and the "rose" directly, but only the idea of the "sun," the idea of the "wormwood," and the idea of the "rose" —and this is what he must mean consistently with his avowed principle that "he knows nothing but his own ideas"—then, is he guilty of "begging the question" when he says he "looks at the sun," he "tastes wormwood" and "smells a rose." For the plain meaning of his words is that he is looking at the actual existing sun, tastes the actually existing wormwood, and smells the actually existing rose. But if this is the obvious meaning of his words, then does the problem which he sets up to solve, vanish. The truth is, that mere vividness of idea is no guarantee or criterion that an actual object corresponding to the idea exists, any more than Descartes' "clearness and distinctness" of an idea is a valid criterion of its actual objectivity.

Locke is bankrupt of proof to establish the actual existence of objects outside of himself by his "way of ideas." He had good intentions. But it is no compliment to his intellectuality to be a realist by profession and an idealist by the force of logic.

That Locke could never get out of himself and know objects outside of his ideas has been the conclusion not only of Berkeley and Hume, who did little more than reduce Locke to logic, but also of more recent English critics of Locke's philosophy, Green and Alexander.

Prof. Archibald Alexander sums up his study of Locke thus:[9] "The truth is that Locke failed to make the transition from the individual to the world, or from the world to the individual. . . . All our knowledge is really subjective according to Locke, and human certainty is only relative certainty."

---

[9]History of Philosophy, pp. 216-217.

Professor Green gives the following estimate of Locke's argument to prove the existence of objects outside of him. He says:[10]

"Only if existence were itself an idea, would the consciousness of the agreement of the idea with it be a case of knowledge; but to make existence an idea is to make the whole question about the agreement of ideas, as such, with existence as such, unmeaning. . . . There can be no assurance of agreement between an idea and that which is no object of consciousness at all. The raising of the question, in fact, as Locke puts it, implies the impossibility of answering it. It cannot be raised with any significance, unless existence is external to, and other than, an idea. It cannot be answered unless existence is, or is given in, an object of consciousness, i.e., an idea."

If, then, knowledge, as Locke explicitly defined it, is the perception of the agreement or disagreement of ideas, it logically follows that when Locke declares "I exist" or "objects outside of me exist," both the subjects "I" and "objects outside of me" and the predicate "exist" are only ideas. Hence it follows that both "his own existence" and the "existence of objects outside of him" are only *idea-existences*, which he could, like Kant think about, but could not know, as actually existing.

It is for these reasons that we are justified in concluding that Locke was logically an idealist, as Kant, speculatively at least, was an idealist.

II

May we not now be justified in pointing out another striking parallelism between Locke and Kant? Though Kant, like Locke, was speculatively an idealist, yet Kant, too, like Locke was also practically a realist. Donat says:[11] "Hence God, immortality, freedom, and the like, (and we may add that ragged urchin of exterior darkness, which Kant called "the-thing-in-itself") remain forever

---

[10]Introduction to Hume's Treatise on Human Nature, sec. 59.
[11]Freedom of Science, p. 44.

outside the field of our theoretical or cognitive reason.
Nevertheless Kant did not like to drop these truths. Hence
he constructed for himself a conviction of another kind.
The "practical reason" is to guide man's action in accom-
plishing the task in which her more timid sister, theoretical reason, failed. And it does it, too. It simply "postulates" these truths; they are its "POSTULATES," since
without them moral life and moral order, which it is
bound to recognize, would be impossible. No one knows,
of course, whether this be truth, but it ought to be truth.
Stat pro ratione voluntas. The Gordian knot is cut. "It
is so," the will now cries from the depths of the soul, "I
believe it"; while the intellect stands hesitatingly by protesting "I don't know whether it is so or not." Doubt and
conviction embrace each other; Yes and No meet peace-
fully. "I had to suspend knowledge," Kant suggests, "in
order to make room for faith" (Kritik der reinen Ver-
nunft, 2. Vorrede.)

In like manner what Locke, the man of common sense
that he was, really declared, as we have proved from intrinsic and extrinsic evidence was—"I don't know whether
objects exist outside of me or not—But I wish that they
exist—I will not have the external world taken from me."

Locke then, could not, as an idealist, make use of any
of the personal pronouns in any legitimate objective
sense. "I," "he," "she" and "it" were for him so many
"ideas" of an unknown "I," "he," "she" and "it." Kant
came, so far as his speculative knowledge extended, to
the same conclusion. But with this difference, that while
Locke should have logically acknowledged that he knew
nothing but "ideas," Kant did avow he could know only
"phenomena." The terms employed, indeed, were different. But were the essences or nature of Locke's "ideas"
different from the essences or nature of Kant's "phenomena?" We venture to affirm that they were not. Kant's
"phenomena" were in their essence or nature sensuous in
so far as they must contain, in order to be known at all,
a sensuous element. So were the ideas of Locke also
sensuous, every one of them, in as much as they too con-

tained a sensuous element. We shall now address ourselves to make good this assertion, and thereby establish the parallelism between the characteristic feature of Locke's "ideas" and Kant's "phenomena." An obvious difficulty will arise in the minds of the readers which would seem to obviate the complete parallelism or likeness between the "ideas" of Locke and the "phenomena" of Kant. Kant's "phenomena" are admittedly an amalgam of subjective sense-impressions plus certain "a priori forms," while Locke's "ideas" seem elementally simple. This difficulty will, I trust, be shorn of its force, when in the last part of this paper, we shall endeavor to show that Locke also superimposed upon his sensuous ideas, what we venture to call interpretatively Locke's "a priori forms" though Locke himself perhaps never distinctly envisaged those "forms" as "a priori."

To discuss each point separately, were all Locke's ideas, which came to him from experience, mere sense-impressions, just as the primary a posteriori "matter" of Kant's phenomena were sense-impressions? That they were, we proceed to make manifest.

We need not labor the argument. That Locke was a sensist is the universal tradition among philosophers. That means, in the case of Locke, that all his experimental ideas, were sensuous. The supersensible was therefore, logically beyond his ken. This position of Locke is borne out by many passages of his "Essay."

Having repudiated innate ideas and innate principles, as he understood them, Locke says: [12] "Let us suppose the mind to be, as we say, white paper, void of all characters, without any ideas. How comes it to be furnished? . . . To this I answer in one word, from EXPERIENCE. In that all our knowledge is founded, and from that it ultimately derives itself."

Then he goes on to say: "Our observation employed about external objects" (sic)—this channel of experience he calls "sensation"—or "about the internal operations of

[12]Bk. II, Ch. I, 2.

our own mind perceived and reflected on by ourselves"—
this second channel of "experience" he calls "reflection"
—"is that which supplies our understanding with all the
materials of thinking. Those two (sensation and reflection) are the fountains of knowledge whence all the ideas
we have, or can naturally have, do spring." This is the
great law which Locke, so to speak, wrote into the Constitution of his Epistemology, to govern the origin of
knowledge for all mankind, namely, that all our knowledge
sprang from "sensation" and "reflection." But we hope
afterwards to show, that notwithstanding his own self-
made law, he literally "bootlegged" in violation of that
law, other elements into his knowledge, that never sprang
from sensation and reflection. But before arriving at that
interesting point of our discussion, our present immediate
purpose is to prove, that all the ideas which Locke derives
through sensation and reflection are sensuous.

Now no one will question, I think, that all the ideas
derived from what Locke calls "sensation" are of their
nature, sensuous. He expressly defines "sensation" as
"an impression or motion made in some part of the
body."[13] Granting that Locke knew he had a body, though
logically he could only know the idea of a body, then those
bodily impressions are certainly sensuous and it is these
sensuous impressions that "produce," as he says, some
perception, that is, some idea in the understanding. For
Locke says:[14] *Having ideas and perception* being the same
thing." Bodily impressions, then *passively* **produce**, i.e.,
cause, in the mind what he calls "ideas of sensation," as
effects. But since the nature of the effect cannot rise
above the nature of the cause, if the cause, i.e., the bodily
impressions, are sensuous, so must the "ideas of sensation" which are the effects. Hence all the ideas derived
from the fountain of "sensation" are of their nature
sensuous.

But what of the ideas derived from "reflection?" Can
we establish that those ideas are also sensuous? Locke

[13]Bk. II, Ch. I, 23.
[14]Bk. II, Ch. I, 9.

explicitly declares that "reflection" has for its objects "the operations of our own mind within us as it is employed about the ideas it has got" from sensation. He writes:[15] "In time the mind comes to reflect on its own operations about the ideas got by sensation, and thereby stores itself with a new set of ideas, which I call ideas of reflection." Now, "the ideas got by sensation" are all sensuous. The operations, consequently, exercised about those sensuous ideas by a faculty which, as Locke himself admits, as we shall presently see, is a sense-faculty, are likewise sensuous. If then, as Locke eloquently maintains,[16] "all those sublime thoughts which tower above the clouds, and reach as high as heaven itself take their rise and footing here: in all that great extent wherein the mind wanders, in those remote speculations it may seem to be elevated with, it stirs not one jot beyond those ideas which sense (sensation) and reflection have offered for its contemplation."

If this is so, then we are constrained to conclude that, according to the mind of Locke, all his experiential ideas, which supply all the materials of his knowledge, are sensuous ideas, or sensuous phenomena, and Locke has anticipated the answer which Kant subsequently had given to his famous question—"What can I know?" Kant embraced Locke across the years. Both knew only subjective experiences which Locke called "ideas," and Kant "phenomena" into which always entered and must enter, sensuous elements.

That the ideas of reflection are sensuous, Locke himself confirms when he explicitly declares that "reflection" is properly a "sense." Locke says:[17] "This source of ideas (reflection) every man has wholly within himself; and though it be not sense, as having nothing to do with external objects, yet it is very like it, and might properly enough be called *internal sense*." It is true that the term

---

[15]Bk. II, Ch. I, 24.
[16]Ibid.
[17]Bk. II, Ch. I, 4.

"sense" is often employed in a peculiar idiomatic use by English philosophers to signify the spiritual faculty of intellect or reason. Newman speaks of the "moral sense" and Hamilton and Reid call the "common reason" of mankind "common sense," because its judgments, by a kind of intellectual instinct, hit off the truth in concrete situations. But this use of the term "sense" is obviously metaphorical or analogous. None of these writers ever call the "moral sense" or "common sense" "properly a sense." This phrase, "properly a sense," which Locke applies to "reflection," precludes, it seems to me, all possibility of designating "reflection" as a sense in a metaphorical or analogous meaning alone. What is "properly a sense" is a sensuous faculty in its own nature and right. Hence, we conclude that Locke's "ideas of sensation" and "ideas of reflection" are all sensuous, or at least, as we shall see presently, like Kant's "phenomena," contain sensuous elements.

III

We now arrive at the discussion, of what perhaps is the most interesting phase of Locke's anticipations of Kant, viz., that Locke while desperately struggling to explain the origin of "substance" and "cause," actually stumbled upon, unconsciously, it may be, such an account of these ideas, as to leave possible no other interpretation, except that which makes these ideas coincide with Kant's theory, that "substance" and "cause" are "a priori forms" derived from the mind itself. Let us first examine Locke's "substance."

Locke, like Kant never got rid of substance, as Berkeley, partially, and Hume, completely, did. "Substance" obsessed Locke and he could not exorcize it from his mind. But he also clearly saw, good sensist that he was, that the idea of "substance" was not and could not be engendered in his mind by any sensuous subjective cluster of ideas which he called an experience, for the simple reason that "substance" as a mode of reality is not and cannot be found directly or indirectly, explicitly or implicitly in any aggregate of isolated subjective ideas and because substance is not a *sensibile per se*. Yet Locke insisted in his controversy with Stillingfleet that substance exists, i.e., it exists in the only way in which Locke, as a logical idealist, could say it exists, i.e., as an idea-existence.

Since Locke, then, could not derive "substance" from any aggregate or cluster of sensuous subjective ideas which was for him an experience, he forthwith, in his desperation, abandons his theory that all ideas are derived from experience, through sensation and reflection, and explains the origin of substance as being derived from within the mind itself, and thus made of it an "a priori form" superimposed upon pure experience, as Kant did.

We can best, perhaps, make good this contention, by quoting from Locke a few concrete examples of what he would call a "complete experience," and then point out, by an analysis of those concrete cases, that at least one of Locke's complete experiences, was like a Kantian complete experience, an amalgam composed of "substance" which arose from within the mind, blended with the matter of his experience, which was an aggregate or cluster of subjective sensuous ideas either of sensation or reflection.

We shall first quote Locke's famous description of a swan. He says:[18]

"Thus the idea (or experience) which an Englishman signifies by the name swan is, white color, long neck, red beak, black legs, and whole feet, and all these of a certain size, with a power of swimming in the water, and making a certain kind of noise, and perhaps, to a man who has long observed this kind of birds, some other properties: which all terminate in sensible simple ideas, *all united in one common subject*!" (Italics ours.)

Analyzing this interesting example, we have, I contend all the requisites which constitute the "matter" and the "a priori form of substance" of Kant's theory, blending together to make this experience of a "swan" possible.

-----
[18]Bk. II, Ch. XXIII, 14.

Of course, Locke does not know the real, actual swan out-side and independent of his ideas of a swan any more than Kant did. He says, explicitly, that all the sensuous swan-qualities of color—"white color," "red beak," "black legs"; and of sound "making a certain noise," which Locke would call "secondary qualities," and all the qualities of exten-sion and power, "long neck," "whole feet," "all of a certain size," "the power of swimming in the water," which he would call "primary qualities," "*all terminate in simple ideas*." They are all subjective and sensuous. This ag-gregate or cluster of simple, subjective, sensuous ideas are the matter of his experience.

But according to Locke there is in addition to these sensuous ideas, another idea, which he expresses by say-ing "all united in one common subject." This one com-mon subject he identifies with "substance," while all the other simple ideas, that constitute the idea of swan, came from pure experience. Whence, we ask, comes this com-mon subject or substance that imparts unity to the whole? Let Locke himself tell us. In his account of the origin of "substance" Locke says:[19]

"The idea then we have, to which we give the *general* name, substance, being nothing but the *supposed* (these italics ours,) but unknown, support, of those qualities we find existing, which we imagine cannot subsist *sine re substante*, without something to support them, we call that support *substantia*; which according to the true im-port of the word is, in plain English, standing under or upholding."

Analyzing this passage, we find in the first place, Locke attributes the origin of substance to a "supposi-tion." Now, when Locke "supposes" substance, from what source does he derive it? Let us see. "To suppose" means to think something that is *determined* by the mind itself, not determined by an object independent of the mind. The object of a "supposition" is *created* by the activity of the mind, not *discovered* by the activity of the mind. Locke's "substance" then, as a mere "supposi-

---
[19]Ibid., 2.

tion" derives its origin from the mind. It certainly cannot be derived from any cluster of subjective sensuous ideas. And that, for two reasons. In the first place, isolated ideas, which are the only objects of Locke's knowledge, are in no sense *substantial*; and, secondly, Locke being a sensist, could not discover substance in any sense-experience as a *sensibile per se*—and substance is not that.

To say, then, that "substance" is a "supposition" can mean nothing else except that "substance" is a creation of the mind. And is not the fact that "substance" is a creation of the mind precisely one of the characteristic features of Kant's "a priori forms?"

Another characteristic feature of Kant's "a priori forms" is *necessity* and consequently *universality*. Necessity in Kant's "a priori forms" consists in this, that all minds, by their present constitution, *must* think them. They are so many grooves along which the mind *must* willy nilly think.

Is Locke's substance furnished with this feature of necessity? We maintain that it is. For Locke explicitly states:[20]

"Hence, when we talk or think of any particular sort of corporeal substance, as horse, stone, etc., though the idea we have of either of them be but the complication or collection of those several simple ideas of sensible qualities, which we used to find united in a thing called horse or stone; yet, *because we cannot conceive how they should subsist alone, nor one in another*, we suppose them existing in, and supported by, some common subject; which support we denote by the name substance."

When Locke in this passage, which he emphasizes by italics, acknowledges that "*we cannot conceive how the collection of several simple ideas of sensible qualities should subsist alone, or in one another*," he came within a hair's breadth of explicitly visioning "substance" as an "a priori form." For the passage "we cannot conceive," etc., implies that we *must* think that the several simple

---

[20]Bk. II, Ch. XXIII, 4.

ideas of sensible qualities are supported and unified by substance. In other words, "substance" is a necessary form of thought springing from the mind. We must think it; we must necessarily suppose it, not because it is really so, in its actual objective existence as a Scholastic would say, but rather it is so, because I must necessarily think it so, which is the Kantian manner of expression. Locke, like Kant, makes the necessity of thinking or supposing "substance" measure and create its object, rather than make the object measure and determine the thought of substance. It is for these reasons that we maintain that Locke invested substance with the feature of subjective necessity which is characteristic of Kant's "a priori forms." Hence, we contend, that the parallelism between Locke's and Kant's explanation of the origin of substance affords sufficient grounds for the conclusion, that Locke at least interpretatively anticipated Kant in formulating the *principle* of "a priori forms" derivable from the mind. If we had no other example except "substance," this example alone would be sufficient to vindicate our claim, that Locke in principle was an "apriorist" as well as Kant.

But this is not the only example. Locke's explanation of the origin of "cause" is another. The origin of this idea was no less perplexing to Locke than was the idea of substance. As a sensuous empiricist, Locke struggled mightily to derive cause from the double fountain of sense-experience: sensation and reflection. He expresses the result of his inquiry in the following passage:[21] "The notion of cause and effect has its rise from ideas received from sensation and reflection." But it is obvious that if "cause" cannot be discovered in experience as a *sensibile per se* of sense, then, it cannot flow through the two channels of experience—sensation and reflection—which convey to the mind what alone is directly sensible in experience. But "cause" is not a *sensibile per se* of sense. The senses whether external or internal, perceive, indeed, certain phenomena uniformly followed by other phenomena. But "cause" contains in its content more elements than

---

[21]Bk. II, Ch. XXVI, 2.

merely antecedent and consequent phenomena. It also embraces in its comprehension efficiency or the power of production. But such modes of reality as these are not the proper or common object of any sense or group of senses. They are not *sensibilia per se*.

Furthermore, there is involved in what begins to exist or happen a necessary and universal relation with some antecedent in order to explain rationally the thing that happens. And surely, sense cannot perceive directly and *per se* necessity and universality. An adequate idea of "cause," then, cannot be derived from experience either by "sensation," which Locke calls the act of the external sense, or by "reflection," which he calls "properly" an internal sense.

Locke, implicitly at least, admitted that all these features—origination, efficiency, necessity and universality—are involved in the notion of "cause," because he professes to reason to the existence of God as Creator, in his "Essay," by means of the principle of causality. Locke, therefore, must have attributed to the Primal Cause of the universe the power of efficient origination of the universe as well as a necessary connection between the things created and the creating cause; and necessity involves universality. Sensuous perception, then, could never directly derive "cause," enriched by so many features, from sense-experience. Hume, as a logical sensist, clearly saw the impossibility of deriving "cause" as a direct object of sense from experience. So he rejected honestly the reality of "cause" and attributed it to custom. Kant also clearly envisaged that "cause" could not be discovered by the senses in experience, so he derived it as an "a priori form" from within the mind.

What did Locke do? He really smuggled intellectual elements into his idea of "cause," in violation of his own expressed law, that all our knowledge comes from sense-experience. For Locke interpreted experience as a sensist must do, in its *formal* signification, that is, he assumed that there is nothing in experience except what is directly and *per se* an object of a sense-faculty. He did not interpret experience, as Scholasticism does, in its *material* signification, namely, that there are other aspects of reality in experience, which though they cannot be directly and *per se* perceived by sense, may be directly and *per se* perceived by intellect.

But whence did Locke derive those intellectual features involved in the notion of "cause"? This is the crux of the question. We contend that Locke again surreptitiously, though perhaps unconsciously, derived all those intellectual features which enrich "cause" from within his mind, as he did in the case of his suppositional "substance." We base this contention on the following passage from Locke, wherein he finally sums up the result of his enquiry into his ideas of "cause."

Locke says:[22] "So that whatever is *considered* by us to conduce or operate to the producing of any particular simple *idea* or collection of simple ideas, whether substance or mode, which did not before exist, hath *thereby in our minds* the relation of a cause, and so is denominated by us." (All italics ours.)

Analyzing this curious passage, what do we glean? The terms "conduce" or "operate to the producing" carry us beyond what is immediately present to the senses or reflection which is "properly" as Locke says, "an internal sense." The senses at least can perceive, in Locke's language, only ideas of phenomenal contiguity and succession. Again Locke in his first letter to Stillingfleet, quoted by Fraser, admits that we are necessitated to think "cause." He says: "Everything that has a beginning *must* have a cause is a true principle of reason, which we come to know by perceiving that *the idea of beginning to be is necessarily connected with the idea of some operation*." We find, therefore, that in addition to the sensuous ideas of the contiguity and succession of phenomena, involved in "cause," Locke smuggled into its idea the intellectually perceived elements of efficiency, origination, and necessity.

Whence did Locke derive these intellectual elements

---

[22] Bk. II, Ch. XXVI, 1.

that go to constitute the adequate idea of a "cause"? Locke, it must be admitted, is rather obscure in his answer. He seems at his wit's end to account for these intellectual elements. As a sensist and idealist he could not discover them as really objective and independent of the mind. So he answers that, that which is *necessary to produce* any particular idea or collection of ideas, which did not exist before, "*hath thereby in our minds the relation of cause.*" Considering Locke's previous explanation of substance as something that sprang from the very constitution of the mind after the manner of an "a priori form," would we be doing violence to this passage of Locke, if we should interpret it in a manner analogous to the interpretation we have given of substance, by saying that Locke observing constant changes and vicissitudes was obliged by the very constitution of his mind to avow that "cause" was a purely mental relation generated by the mind itself—"*hath thereby in our minds the relation of cause?*" Locke does not say that "the relation of cause" exists between the simple sensuous ideas, the only objects he knows, nor does he say that "the relation of cause" is grounded on objects external to, and independent of the mind, but like Kant, he declares, "that whatever is considered by us (notice the word 'considered,' i.e., thought of by us) to conduce or operate to the producing any particular simple idea, whether substance or mode, which did not exist before, *hath thereby in our minds the relation of cause.*" This seems to imply that "the relation of cause" is generated by a necessity of thought by the mind itself and then superimposed upon the sensuous ideas or sense-experiences of the antecedent and consequent as an "a priori form," and thereby constituting a compound or amalgam that becomes a complete phenomenal experience as Kant would say.

IV

To sum up, then, the conclusions we have arrived at in this little study of the affinities between Locke and Kant, we submit:

1. That like Kant, Locke, though he professed Realism, was logically an Idealist.

2. That Locke's ideas were, every one of them, professedly at least sensuous. Locke, explicitly states:[23] that "every man's reasoning and knowledge is only about the ideas existing in his own mind; which are truly, every one of them, particular existences. . . . So that the perception of the agreement or disagreement of our particular ideas is the whole and utmost of our knowledge." Hence Locke's ideas are all sensuous phenomena and the "whole and utmost" of his knowledge is confined like Kant to sensuous phenomena. Yet despite this avowal Locke seems to have surreptitiously smuggled into his mind some pure intellectual ideas.

3. We have attempted to make manifest that Locke's account of the origin of "substance" and "cause" may be interpreted as arising necessarily from the constitution of his own mind, thereby establishing that Locke, at least in principle, anticipated the "a priori forms" of Kant.

4. Lastly, though the whole tendency of Locke's philosophy was sensistic, yet it may be truthfully maintained that Locke was not a thorough-going sensist. He was a sensist as Kant was a sensist.

---

[23]Bk. IV, Ch. XXVII, 8.